TAINTED WATERS

INTERNATIONAL LAWS RESPONSE TO OIL AND GAS

AMAKA EKPECHAM

TAINTED WATERS

International Laws Response To Oil And Gas

Amaka Ekpecham

TABLE OF CONTENTS

CHAPTER 1
INTRODUCTION TO OIL AND GAS SPILLAGES

- **The Environmental and Economic Impact of Spillages**

The occurrence of oil and gas spillages in our oceans and ecosystems presents a pressing concern, with far-reaching consequences for both the environment and the global economy. These incidents, whether resulting from offshore drilling, transportation, or industrial processes, can cause significant harm to the delicate balance of our ecosystems and exert substantial economic burdens.

Environmental Impact:

1. **Ecosystem Disruption:** Oil and gas spillages pose a severe threat to marine ecosystems. When a spill occurs, it releases a complex mixture of hydrocarbons, including crude oil and refined petroleum products, into the environment. These substances are highly toxic to aquatic life, causing immediate and long-term damage. Crude oil, in particular, contains various compounds, such as polycyclic aromatic hydrocarbons (PAHs), that can be lethal to fish, birds, and marine mammals. The smothering and

contamination of aquatic life disrupt the natural balance of ecosystems.

2. **Water Quality:** Oil spillages lead to the formation of oil slicks on the water's surface, which have far-reaching implications for water quality. These slicks block sunlight from penetrating the water, reducing the availability of light for photosynthetic organisms such as phytoplankton and aquatic plants. Furthermore, oil films limit the exchange of oxygen between the atmosphere and the water, resulting in decreased oxygen levels in affected areas. Low oxygen levels can lead to hypoxia, creating "dead zones" where marine life struggles to survive.

3. **Biodiversity Loss:** The toxic constituents of oil have the potential to cause harm to a wide range of species, from microscopic plankton to large marine mammals. PAHs and other chemical components of oil can disrupt the reproduction and development of aquatic organisms. This can lead to reduced population sizes, genetic mutations, and an overall loss of biodiversity. Spillages can also have cascading effects through the food web, impacting species that rely on the affected organisms for food.

4. **Habitat Destruction:** Coastal habitats, such as marshes, mangroves, and coral reefs, are particularly vulnerable to oil and gas contamination. These habitats serve as nurseries and breeding grounds for many species. Oil spillages can smother these fragile environments, destroying critical breeding sites and reducing the

availability of shelter and food for young marine life. The long-lasting effects of habitat destruction can result in profound ecological changes.

5. **Global Impact:** Oil and gas spillages have global implications due to the interconnected nature of marine ecosystems. Oceans play a crucial role in regulating the Earth's climate, absorbing carbon dioxide, and providing sustenance for billions of people. When oil contaminates the oceans, it disrupts these critical functions. Reduced photosynthesis and altered ocean chemistry can affect the global carbon cycle and contribute to climate change. Additionally, the contamination of marine resources can impact food security and livelihoods worldwide.

Economic Impact:

1. **Direct Cleanup Costs:** Responding to oil and gas spillages is a costly endeavor. Governments, companies, and environmental organizations must allocate substantial resources for immediate cleanup efforts. This includes deploying specialized equipment and personnel, such as oil skimmers, booms, and cleanup crews. The cost of containment, recovery, and disposal of spilled oil can run into the millions or even billions of dollars.

2. **Loss of Revenue:** The industries most directly impacted by oil and gas spillages are often fisheries and tourism. Contaminated waters can lead to fishery closures, resulting in financial losses for fishermen and seafood businesses. In coastal areas reliant on

tourism, the visible environmental damage can deter visitors, leading to a decline in tourism revenues and job losses.

3. **Healthcare Costs:** The exposure to hazardous substances released during oil spillages can result in health issues for local communities. Individuals in affected areas may experience respiratory problems, skin diseases, and other health complications. Addressing these health issues requires additional healthcare resources and can lead to higher healthcare costs.

4. **Litigation and Compensation:** Companies responsible for oil and gas spillages frequently face legal action and may be required to provide compensation to affected parties. Legal battles can be protracted, costly, and result in substantial settlements. Compensation may be directed towards environmental restoration, health and medical expenses, and economic losses experienced by local communities.

5. **Long-Term Economic Impact:** The economic repercussions of oil and gas spillages can be felt for years, if not decades, after the incident. Impaired ecosystems, reduced productivity in affected regions, and decreased property values can hinder economic growth and exacerbate social and economic disparities. The recovery process often necessitates substantial investments in habitat restoration and ecosystem rehabilitation.

In conclusion, oil and gas spillages exact a significant toll on both the environment and the global economy. Efforts to prevent these incidents, as well as strategies for swift and effective response and recovery, are of paramount importance. Moreover, long-term measures to reduce our dependence on fossil fuels and transition to more sustainable energy sources are vital in mitigating the environmental and economic consequences of oil and gas spillages.

- **The Human Toll of Oil and Gas Spillages**

Direct Health Impacts:

1. **Physical Health Effects:** Oil and gas spillages can have immediate health consequences for individuals exposed to the toxic substances. Contact with crude oil and its components can result in skin rashes, burns, and respiratory problems. In severe cases, inhalation of volatile organic compounds (VOCs) released from spilled oil can lead to more serious health conditions, including nausea, headaches, and dizziness.

2. **Psychological Stress:** Spillages can cause psychological distress among affected individuals and communities. The loss of livelihoods, contamination of homes, and witnessing the environmental devastation can lead to anxiety, depression, and post-traumatic stress disorder (PTSD). Communities facing protracted cleanup and recovery efforts may experience ongoing psychological stress.

3.   **Long-Term Health Effects:** Some health effects may not manifest immediately but develop over time. Prolonged exposure to oil and its byproducts can lead to chronic health problems, such as respiratory diseases, cardiovascular issues, and various forms of cancer. Individuals involved in cleanup and response efforts are particularly at risk due to repeated exposure to hazardous materials.

Social and Economic Impacts:

1.   **Loss of Livelihoods:** Fishing communities and tourism-dependent areas often bear the brunt of oil and gas spillages. Fishermen may face extensive closures of fishing grounds, resulting in income loss. Tourism-based businesses, from hotels to restaurants, may experience a drop in visitors due to the environmental damage. As a result, local economies can suffer, and communities may struggle to make ends meet.

2.   **Displacement and Relocation:** In some cases, the severity of a spill may necessitate the temporary or permanent displacement of communities. Residents forced to leave their homes experience disruptions in their lives and communities, with social ties strained and cultural heritage at risk of erosion.

3.   **Healthcare Costs:** Communities affected by oil and gas spillages often incur healthcare expenses related to the treatment of spill-related illnesses and health conditions. Individuals may need medical care for respiratory issues, skin problems, and mental health

challenges. These expenses can strain local healthcare systems and individual finances.

Environmental Justice and Vulnerable Communities:

1. **Disproportionate Impact:** Vulnerable and marginalized communities, including Indigenous populations and low-income neighborhoods, often suffer the most from oil and gas spillages. These communities are more likely to be located near oil and gas infrastructure and are less equipped to cope with the consequences of spills. The disproportionate impact on these communities raises concerns about environmental justice.

2. **Cultural and Subsistence Disruption:** Indigenous communities that rely on traditional practices, such as fishing, hunting, and gathering, can experience the disruption of their subsistence lifestyle due to spillages. This not only affects their access to food but also their cultural identity and way of life.

Community Resilience and Response:

1. **Community Organizing:** In the aftermath of oil and gas spillages, affected communities often mobilize to advocate for their rights, demand compensation, and participate in decision-making processes related to cleanup and recovery efforts. Community organizations and activists play a crucial role in raising awareness and holding responsible parties accountable.

2.   **Healthcare and Mental Health Services:** Responding to the human toll of spillages involves providing healthcare services, mental health support, and resources for affected individuals and communities. Initiatives like mobile health clinics and mental health counseling can aid in addressing immediate and long-term health impacts.

In conclusion, oil and gas spillages have a significant human toll, ranging from immediate health effects to long-term consequences. The social and economic impacts are profound, particularly in vulnerable communities. Addressing the human toll of spillages requires a multi-faceted approach, including preventive measures, robust response systems, and support for affected individuals and communities.

- **The Evolution of Environmental Awareness**

Pre-Industrial Era:

1.   **Harmony with Nature:** In ancient and indigenous societies, there was often a deep sense of harmony with nature. People recognized their dependence on the environment for survival and believed in maintaining a respectful balance with the natural world. This relationship was often guided by spiritual beliefs and traditional ecological knowledge.

Industrial Revolution and Early Conservation:

2. **Industrialization and Urbanization:** The Industrial Revolution brought significant technological advances but also environmental degradation. Rapid urbanization and the growth of industries led to pollution, deforestation, and habitat destruction. Early conservationists, like John Muir and Henry David Thoreau, emerged to advocate for the preservation of natural landscapes.

Early 20th Century:

3. **National Parks and Environmental Legislation:** The early 20th century saw the creation of national parks in various countries, including the establishment of the National Park Service in the United States. This era also marked the inception of environmental legislation, such as the U.S. National Environmental Policy Act (NEPA) in 1969.

Mid-20th Century:

4. **Silent Spring and Modern Environmentalism:** Rachel Carson's groundbreaking book "Silent Spring," published in 1962, raised public awareness about the harmful effects of pesticides and is often credited with sparking the modern environmental movement. This led to the establishment of environmental organizations and the first Earth Day in 1970.

Late 20th Century:

5.   **Global Environmental Issues:** In the late 20th century, global environmental issues gained prominence. The 1987 Brundtland Report introduced the concept of sustainable development. Concerns about ozone depletion led to the Montreal Protocol, while climate change became a pressing issue, culminating in the United Nations Framework Convention on Climate Change (UNFCCC) in 1992.

21st Century:

6.   **Technological Advancements:** The 21st century has seen a surge in technology that enables real-time sharing of environmental information. This includes satellite imagery, online platforms for environmental data, and social media, which has allowed for the rapid dissemination of environmental news and activism.

7.   **Climate Change Awareness:** Climate change has become a central focus of environmental awareness. The Intergovernmental Panel on Climate Change (IPCC) and initiatives like the Paris Agreement have brought global attention to the urgent need to address climate-related challenges.

Current Trends:

8.   **Biodiversity Conservation:** Awareness of biodiversity loss and the importance of conserving ecosystems has grown. Efforts to

protect endangered species and conserve habitats are part of contemporary environmental discourse.

9. **Environmental Justice:** Environmental awareness now includes a focus on environmental justice, recognizing that vulnerable communities are disproportionately affected by environmental issues. This has led to calls for equitable solutions and a more inclusive environmental movement.

10. **Youth-Led Movements:** Young activists, exemplified by figures like Greta Thunberg, have taken center stage in advocating for climate action and environmental sustainability. Youth-led movements have brought fresh energy to environmental awareness and activism.

In conclusion, the evolution of environmental awareness is marked by a transition from traditional harmony with nature to a global movement for environmental protection and sustainability. This journey is shaped by scientific discoveries, technological advancements, advocacy efforts, and a growing understanding of the interconnectedness of human well-being and the health of the planet.

- **The Necessity of International Cooperation**

1. **Global Environmental Challenges:** The 21st century has brought about a growing awareness of the interconnectedness of environmental challenges. Climate change, biodiversity loss,

transboundary air and water pollution, and the management of shared resources are global issues that transcend national borders. No single nation can address these challenges effectively in isolation.

2. **Shared Responsibility:** Environmental problems often have transnational causes and consequences. For instance, greenhouse gas emissions from one country contribute to global climate change that affects the entire planet. International cooperation recognizes the shared responsibility in addressing these challenges and the need for collective action.

3. **Mitigating Environmental Conflicts:** International cooperation is essential to prevent and resolve conflicts arising from environmental issues. Competing claims over water resources, disputes related to transboundary pollution, or conflicts over access to shared fisheries necessitate diplomatic negotiations and agreements to prevent hostilities.

4. **Scientific Collaboration:** International cooperation fosters scientific research and data sharing, which are critical for understanding and addressing global environmental challenges. Collaborative efforts between scientists from different countries lead to a deeper understanding of the environment and the development of effective solutions.

5.   **Legal Frameworks:** International agreements and treaties provide legal frameworks for the sustainable management of shared resources and the regulation of activities with global environmental impacts. Treaties like the Paris Agreement and the Convention on Biological Diversity establish norms and commitments that guide national policies and actions.

6.   **Disaster Response and Relief:** Natural disasters, such as oil spills and nuclear accidents, do not respect national boundaries. International cooperation is vital for coordinating emergency responses and providing relief and assistance to affected regions. Agreements like the International Convention on Oil Pollution Preparedness, Response, and Co-operation (OPRC) facilitate such cooperation.

7.   **Trade and Environmental Standards:** International cooperation is needed to establish and enforce environmental standards in global trade. Agreements like the Basel Convention on the Control of Transboundary Movements of Hazardous Wastes and their Disposal aim to regulate the movement and disposal of hazardous waste to prevent environmental harm.

8.   **Capacity Building and Technology Transfer:** Developing countries often lack the resources and technology needed to address environmental challenges effectively. International cooperation includes capacity-building initiatives and the transfer of technology,

knowledge, and financial resources to assist these countries in their sustainability efforts.

9. **Diplomacy and Negotiation:** Environmental issues frequently involve complex negotiations among multiple parties with diverse interests. Diplomacy and international forums, such as the United Nations, facilitate dialogue and consensus-building, leading to the adoption of international agreements and protocols.

10. **Global Resilience:** Global environmental challenges, including pandemics and climate change, affect the resilience of nations and societies. International cooperation strengthens the ability of countries to respond collectively, share knowledge and resources, and build a more resilient and sustainable future.

In conclusion, international cooperation is not a choice but a necessity in addressing the complex, interconnected environmental challenges of our time. It requires nations to recognize their shared responsibility, engage in diplomatic efforts, and work together to develop and implement solutions that benefit the global community and safeguard the planet for future generations.

- **Who can use this Book?**

The book, "The Role of International Law in Addressing Oil and Gas Spillages," can be a valuable resource for a diverse range of individuals and groups, including:

1.   **Environmental Professionals:** Environmental scientists, researchers, and policymakers can use the book to gain insights into the legal frameworks and international cooperation required to address oil and gas spillages effectively.

2.   **Government Officials:** Government officials, particularly those involved in environmental ministries and international relations, can benefit from the book's information on international treaties, agreements, and best practices for addressing environmental crises.

3.   **Legal Professionals:** Lawyers, judges, and legal scholars interested in international environmental law will find the book a valuable reference for understanding the legal aspects of oil and gas spillages.

4.   **Business and Industry:** Oil and gas companies, as well as businesses involved in related industries, can use the book to gain an understanding of their responsibilities, liabilities, and best practices in environmental protection.

5.   **Non-Governmental Organizations (NGOs):** Environmental and humanitarian NGOs can use the book to educate themselves about the international legal mechanisms available to advocate for environmental protection and the rights of affected communities.

6.   **Educators and Students:** The book can serve as a textbook or supplementary reading material for courses in environmental law, international relations, environmental science, and related fields.

7.   **Community Advocates:** Individuals and community groups affected by or concerned about oil and gas spillages can use the book to better understand their rights and avenues for advocacy and action.

8.   **Global Policymakers:** International organizations and policymakers, such as the United Nations, can use the book as a reference to inform policy discussions and negotiations related to environmental protection.

9.   **General Public:** Informed citizens interested in the environmental impact of oil and gas spillages and the role of international law can gain valuable knowledge and insight from the book.

10. **Researchers and Scholars:** Academics conducting research in the areas of international environmental law, environmental ethics, and the sociology of environmental issues can use the book to explore a comprehensive overview of the subject matter.

The book is designed to provide a broad perspective on the complex issues surrounding oil and gas spillages, making it accessible and informative for a wide audience interested in understanding and addressing these environmental challenges from a legal and international cooperation standpoint.

CHAPTER 2
INTERNATIONAL LEGAL FRAMEWORKS FOR OIL AND GAS SPILLAGES

- **Treaty-Based Approaches**

1. **Defining Treaty-Based Approaches:** Treaty-based approaches refer to the use of international agreements or treaties as legal instruments to address specific environmental challenges, such as oil and gas spillages. These treaties set out the rights, responsibilities, and obligations of the parties involved, often nations, in managing and mitigating the impact of such incidents.

2. **Key Environmental Treaties:** Various international environmental treaties and conventions play a crucial role in regulating activities related to oil and gas extraction, transportation, and spill response. Examples include the United Nations Convention on the Law of the Sea (UNCLOS), the International Convention for the Prevention of Pollution from Ships (MARPOL), and the Basel Convention on the Control of Transboundary Movements of Hazardous Wastes.

3. **UNCLOS and the EEZ:** UNCLOS is a fundamental treaty governing activities in the world's oceans. It establishes the Exclusive Economic Zone (EEZ), which grants coastal states jurisdiction over natural resources within 200 nautical miles of their

coastlines. UNCLOS contains provisions related to marine pollution, including oil spills, and sets the framework for liability and compensation.

4. **MARPOL and Shipping Pollution:** The MARPOL Convention addresses pollution from ships, including oil pollution. It establishes regulations to prevent pollution from ships, requiring the use of specific equipment and procedures to minimize the risk of oil spills. MARPOL also outlines response measures in the event of a spill.

5. **Basel Convention on Hazardous Wastes:** The Basel Convention aims to control and manage the transboundary movement of hazardous waste, including waste generated by the oil and gas industry. This treaty establishes rules for the export and import of hazardous waste and ensures that it is handled and disposed of safely.

6. **Regional Environmental Agreements:** In addition to global treaties, regional agreements play a significant role in addressing environmental challenges. For example, the OSPAR Convention focuses on the protection of the marine environment in the Northeast Atlantic, addressing oil spills and other pollution concerns in the region.

7. **Bilateral and Multilateral Agreements:** Beyond multilateral treaties, countries often engage in bilateral or

multilateral agreements with neighboring nations to address specific environmental issues, such as shared water bodies, pipelines, or joint emergency response plans for oil and gas spillages.

8. **Legal Obligations and Enforcement:** Treaty-based approaches create legal obligations for signatory countries, which are bound to comply with the provisions of the treaty. Enforcement mechanisms, such as dispute resolution mechanisms and compliance committees, ensure that parties fulfill their commitments.

9. **Compensation and Liability:** Many environmental treaties, including those related to oil and gas spillages, address issues of liability and compensation for damages. This ensures that those responsible for environmental harm bear the financial burden of cleanup and restoration.

10. **Evolving International Law:** Treaty-based approaches are not static; they evolve in response to new challenges and scientific understanding. As environmental awareness grows and new technologies emerge, international treaties adapt to address emerging issues related to oil and gas spillages and other environmental concerns.

In conclusion, treaty-based approaches are a cornerstone of international efforts to address environmental issues, including oil and gas spillages. These legally binding agreements provide a framework for international cooperation, dispute resolution, and the implementation of measures to protect the environment and promote sustainability.

- **Customary International Law**

Exploring "Customary International Law" and its relevance in addressing environmental issues like oil and gas spillages:

1. **Defining Customary International Law:** Customary international law is a fundamental source of international law that arises from the consistent and general practice of states, followed by a belief in the legal obligation to adhere to such practices. Customary law is binding on all states, irrespective of whether they are parties to specific treaties.

2. **Customary Law in Environmental Context:** Customary international law plays a significant role in the context of environmental protection, including addressing oil and gas spillages. It provides legal norms and principles that guide state behavior and expectations regarding environmental responsibilities.

3. **State Practice in Environmental Protection:** State practice in the field of environmental protection, such as adopting regulations, participating in international agreements, and implementing pollution prevention measures, contributes to the formation of customary environmental norms.

4. **Examples of Customary Environmental Norms:** Customary international law has given rise to several environmental norms. For example, the duty to prevent transboundary harm, including environmental damage caused by oil and gas spillages, is considered a customary norm. This duty requires states to take measures to prevent environmental harm that could affect other states.

5. **Principles of Prevention and Due Diligence:** Customary international law reflects the principles of prevention and due diligence. States are expected to take proactive measures to prevent environmental harm, and failure to do so can lead to state responsibility and liability for damages resulting from oil and gas spillages.

6. **International Court Decisions:** Decisions of international courts and tribunals, such as the International Court of Justice (ICJ), can contribute to the development of customary environmental law. Precedents set by these institutions often shape state practice and expectations.

7. **Persistent Objector Doctrine:** Customary international law is not automatically binding on states that persistently object to a specific practice or norm. However, states must demonstrate their persistent objection and refusal to accept the norm.

8. **Jus Cogens and Environmental Norms:** Some environmental norms may rise to the level of peremptory norms or

jus cogens, which are fundamental principles of international law that cannot be violated. Violations of jus cogens norms, such as environmental principles that protect the well-being of the global environment, can have serious consequences.

9. **State Responsibility and Liability:** Customary international law principles, combined with state practice, establish the basis for state responsibility and liability when environmental harm occurs due to activities related to oil and gas extraction and transportation. States can be held accountable for breaches of customary environmental norms.

10. **Evolution of Customary Law:** Customary international law is not static; it evolves over time as state practice and opinio juris (the belief that a practice is legally required) change in response to emerging environmental challenges, scientific understanding, and societal expectations.

In conclusion, customary international law is a critical element in addressing environmental issues like oil and gas spillages. It provides a foundation of legal norms and principles that guide state behavior and foster international cooperation in environmental protection. Customary environmental law complements treaty-based approaches and helps ensure that states adhere to their environmental responsibilities.

- **Regional Agreements**

Exploring "Regional Agreements" in the context of addressing oil and gas spillages and environmental protection:

1. **Definition of Regional Agreements:** Regional agreements are legally binding pacts between a group of countries within a specific geographical region. These agreements are designed to address shared concerns and challenges, including those related to the environment.

2. **Regional Environmental Agreements:** In the context of environmental protection, regional agreements focus on issues that are specific to a particular region. They are often tailored to the unique environmental, social, and economic characteristics of the region.

3. **Relevance of Regional Agreements:** Regional agreements are crucial for addressing environmental challenges, such as oil and gas spillages, for several reasons:

- **Tailored Solutions:** They allow countries within a region to develop solutions that are better suited to their specific circumstances, taking into account local ecosystems and vulnerabilities.

- **Proximity and Shared Resources:** Countries in a region often share common ecosystems, rivers, seas, or airsheds. Regional agreements facilitate cooperation in the management of shared resources and in responding to environmental incidents like oil spills.

- **Cultural and Socioeconomic Similarities:** Regional agreements can build on common cultural and socioeconomic ties among neighboring countries, making it easier to establish trust and collaboration.

- **Operational Efficiency:** Regional agreements can streamline administrative processes, such as inspections, information sharing, and response mechanisms, leading to more effective and efficient management of environmental issues.

4. **Examples of Regional Environmental Agreements:** There are various regional environmental agreements worldwide. Some examples include:

- **The OSPAR Convention:** Focused on protecting the marine environment of the North-East Atlantic, the OSPAR Convention addresses oil and gas pollution, as well as other maritime concerns.

- **The Arctic Council:** Comprising eight Arctic nations, the Arctic Council focuses on environmental protection, including measures to address oil spills and other environmental threats in the Arctic region.

- **The Regional Seas Program:** Implemented by the United Nations Environment Programme (UNEP), this program fosters cooperation among countries in defined regional seas areas to address marine pollution, including oil spills.

- **The Aarhus Convention:** Focused on public participation in environmental decision-making, the Aarhus Convention operates regionally in Europe to promote transparency and access to environmental information.

5. **Key Components of Regional Agreements:** Regional environmental agreements typically include provisions for:

- **Environmental Monitoring:** Establishing systems for monitoring the state of the environment within the region.

- **Prevention Measures:** Outlining preventive measures to minimize the risk of environmental harm, such as oil and gas spillages.

- **Response Mechanisms:** Defining protocols and response mechanisms for addressing environmental incidents when they occur, including cleanup and restoration efforts.

- **Capacity Building:** Promoting the development of technical and administrative capacities among member states to effectively manage environmental challenges.

- **Information Exchange:** Facilitating the sharing of data, research findings, and best practices among member states.

- **Dispute Resolution:** Establishing mechanisms for resolving disputes related to environmental issues within the region.

6. **Challenges and Benefits:** Regional agreements offer numerous benefits, but they can also face challenges, such as the need for harmonization with national laws and regulations, ensuring compliance, and securing adequate resources for implementation. However, these agreements remain critical tools in addressing environmental concerns like oil and gas spillages in a context that considers regional specificities.

In conclusion, regional agreements are vital for addressing environmental challenges, including oil and gas spillages, within specific geographic areas. They provide a platform for countries to work collaboratively, share responsibilities, and tailor solutions to address environmental threats that affect their shared ecosystems and communities.

- **Bilateral Agreements**

Exploring "Bilateral Agreements" and their role in addressing environmental issues, including oil and gas spillages:

1. **Definition of Bilateral Agreements:** Bilateral agreements, also known as bilateral treaties or agreements between two parties, are legal pacts established between two nations to address specific issues or concerns of mutual interest. In the context of environmental protection, these agreements focus on collaborative

efforts to manage shared resources and mitigate environmental risks.

2. **Relevance of Bilateral Agreements in Environmental Protection:**

- **Resource Management:** Bilateral agreements are crucial when two countries share common ecosystems, water bodies, or airsheds. They provide a framework for jointly managing and protecting these shared resources, particularly in situations involving oil and gas extraction and transportation.

- **Transboundary Environmental Issues:** Countries often face transboundary environmental challenges, such as oil spills or air pollution, that can impact neighboring nations. Bilateral agreements allow for coordinated responses to such issues.

- **Conflict Resolution:** These agreements help prevent and resolve disputes over environmental issues, ensuring peaceful and cooperative management of shared resources.

- **Risk Mitigation:** Bilateral agreements facilitate the development of contingency plans and response mechanisms to address environmental incidents like oil and gas spillages. They ensure both nations are prepared to respond effectively.

- **Data and Information Sharing:** These agreements enable the exchange of environmental data, scientific research, and best practices, enhancing cooperation in environmental monitoring and decision-making.

3. **Components of Bilateral Agreements in Environmental Protection:**

- **Resource Management:** Bilateral agreements outline principles and measures for sustainable resource management, setting rules for responsible resource extraction and ensuring equitable benefits for both countries.

- **Environmental Impact Assessment:** They may require joint environmental impact assessments for projects that could affect both nations, ensuring that potential environmental harm is identified and mitigated.

- **Prevention and Response Protocols:** Bilateral agreements typically define preventive measures and response protocols for environmental incidents. This may include provisions for sharing resources and responsibilities in the event of oil spills.

- **Dispute Resolution:** These agreements establish mechanisms for dispute resolution, should disagreements arise in the implementation of environmental commitments.

- **Collaborative Research and Data Sharing:** They encourage joint research initiatives and data sharing to enhance environmental monitoring and management.

4. **Examples of Bilateral Environmental Agreements:**

•	**U.S.-Canada Agreement on Air Quality:** This agreement between the United States and Canada addresses transboundary air pollution, setting limits on emissions of pollutants that affect air quality in both countries.

•	**Norway-Russia Fisheries Agreements:** These agreements regulate fishing in shared waters and are aimed at sustainable fisheries management to protect marine ecosystems.

•	**U.S.-Mexico Border Environmental Cooperation Agreement:** Focusing on the border region between the United States and Mexico, this agreement addresses various environmental issues, including water quality and waste management.

5. **Benefits and Challenges of Bilateral Agreements:**

•	**Benefits:** Bilateral agreements offer tailored solutions for specific environmental issues, enabling countries to collaborate closely, promote shared responsibility, and respond more effectively to transboundary challenges.

•	**Challenges:** Challenges may include differences in legal frameworks, enforcement mechanisms, and resource disparities between the two parties. Effective implementation and compliance can be complex.

6. **Adaptability:** Bilateral agreements can evolve over time to address emerging environmental challenges and changes in the

environmental landscape. They provide flexibility in responding to new concerns, such as advancements in oil and gas extraction technology or changes in environmental regulations.

In conclusion, bilateral agreements are essential tools for addressing environmental issues, including oil and gas spillages, between two neighboring countries. They enable cooperative management of shared resources and facilitate the prevention, response, and resolution of environmental challenges, promoting sustainability and environmental protection across borders.

- **Regulatory Gaps and Challenges**

Exploring "Regulatory Gaps and Challenges" in the context of addressing oil and gas spillages and environmental protection:

1. **Regulatory Gaps:** Regulatory gaps refer to the inadequacies or limitations in existing legal frameworks and regulations that fail to address specific environmental issues comprehensively. In the context of oil and gas spillages, regulatory gaps can lead to gaps in preparedness, response, and liability.

2. **Complexity of Environmental Systems:** Environmental systems are complex, interconnected, and often span international borders. Regulatory frameworks may struggle to address the intricacies of ecosystems and pollution dynamics, making it challenging to prevent and respond to oil and gas spillages effectively.

3. **Transboundary Pollution:** Oil and gas spillages often involve transboundary pollution, where the impact extends beyond national borders. Regulatory gaps may exist in terms of transboundary liability, compensation mechanisms, and enforcement, making it difficult to hold responsible parties accountable.

4. **Rapid Technological Advancements:** The oil and gas industry constantly evolves with new technologies and practices. Regulatory frameworks may lag behind, failing to adapt to emerging risks and challenges associated with these advancements.

5. **Inadequate Monitoring and Reporting:** Regulatory gaps may occur when monitoring and reporting requirements for oil and gas activities are insufficient. Incomplete or inaccurate data can hinder the assessment of environmental impact and the development of effective regulations.

6. **Enforcement and Compliance:** Regulatory gaps can result from inadequate enforcement mechanisms and challenges in ensuring compliance with environmental regulations. Weak enforcement can lead to a culture of non-compliance, putting the environment at risk.

7. **Overlapping and Conflicting Regulations:** Conflicting or overlapping regulations at the national and international levels can create regulatory gaps, making it unclear which legal framework

takes precedence. Such conflicts can lead to confusion and challenges in enforcement.

8. **Legal Jurisdiction and Responsibility:** Determining legal jurisdiction and responsibility for oil and gas spillages can be complicated, especially in international waters or areas with overlapping claims. Regulatory gaps in defining jurisdiction can hinder response efforts and liability assignment.

9. **Scientific Uncertainty:** The scientific understanding of the long-term environmental impacts of oil and gas spillages continues to evolve. Regulatory gaps may emerge when regulations are based on outdated scientific knowledge or do not adequately account for uncertainties.

10. **Public Participation and Access to Justice:** Ensuring public participation and access to justice in environmental matters is essential. Regulatory gaps can exist when legal frameworks do not sufficiently support the involvement of affected communities and individuals in decision-making processes.

11. **Socioeconomic Considerations:** Environmental regulations should also consider socioeconomic factors, especially in vulnerable communities. Failure to address these concerns can create regulatory gaps in achieving equitable and just outcomes in the aftermath of oil and gas spillages.

12. **Global Cooperation and Enforcement:** International cooperation and enforcement of environmental regulations are essential for addressing oil and gas spillages that span multiple countries. Regulatory gaps can emerge when countries do not collaborate effectively or when enforcement mechanisms are weak.

13. **Emerging Risks:** Regulatory gaps can arise from new, unforeseen risks related to oil and gas activities, such as deep-sea drilling or the development of unconventional fossil fuel resources. Regulations may not have anticipated these risks, leaving gaps in oversight.

Addressing regulatory gaps and challenges requires continuous monitoring and adaptation of legal frameworks to keep pace with changing environmental and industrial landscapes. It also involves international cooperation, transparent governance, and a commitment to protecting the environment and the well-being of communities affected by oil and gas spillages.

CHAPTER 3

THE UNITED NATIONS CONVENTION ON THE LAW OF THE SEA (UNCLOS)

- **Key Provisions of UNCLOS**

The United Nations Convention on the Law of the Sea (UNCLOS) is a comprehensive international treaty that governs the use of the world's oceans and resources. It plays a crucial role in the management and protection of marine environments, including addressing issues related to oil and gas spillages. Here are some key provisions of UNCLOS:

1. **Territorial Sea:** UNCLOS establishes the concept of a territorial sea, which extends 12 nautical miles from a coastal state's baseline. Coastal states have full sovereignty over their territorial sea, including the seabed and subsoil.

2. **Exclusive Economic Zone (EEZ):** Coastal states have exclusive rights to explore and exploit the natural resources within an EEZ, which extends up to 200 nautical miles from their baselines. This includes fisheries and potentially oil and gas resources. However, other states enjoy the freedom of navigation and overflight in the EEZ.

3.   **Continental Shelf:** UNCLOS defines the continental shelf as the seabed and subsoil of the submarine areas adjacent to the coast. Coastal states have sovereign rights over the continental shelf for the purpose of exploring and exploiting its natural resources, including oil and gas deposits.

4.   **High Seas:** UNCLOS establishes that the high seas are open to all states, and no state can exercise sovereignty over them. This includes freedom of navigation, overflight, fishing, and scientific research on the high seas.

5.   **Protection of the Marine Environment:** UNCLOS includes provisions for the protection and preservation of the marine environment. This includes measures to prevent and control marine pollution, including oil spills.

6.   **Marine Pollution:** The treaty sets guidelines for the prevention, reduction, and control of marine pollution, including provisions related to oil pollution. States are obligated to cooperate to prevent, control, and mitigate the effects of pollution incidents.

7.   **Liability for Pollution Damage:** UNCLOS establishes liability for oil pollution damage and compensation for affected states. The "polluter pays" principle holds operators responsible for pollution incidents.

8. **Freedom of Navigation:** UNCLOS ensures the freedom of navigation, including the right of innocent passage through territorial seas and archipelagic waters.

9. **Archipelagic States:** Archipelagic states have sovereignty over their waters enclosed by straight baselines, and they may claim archipelagic sea lanes and air routes. However, these sea lanes must be designated to ensure freedom of navigation.

10. **Deep Seabed Mining:** UNCLOS established the International Seabed Authority to regulate deep seabed mining activities beyond national jurisdiction. It ensures that mining activities are conducted for the benefit of humankind and with minimal environmental impact.

11. **Dispute Settlement:** The treaty includes mechanisms for dispute settlement, allowing parties to resolve disputes through negotiation, arbitration, or recourse to the International Court of Justice.

12. **Marine Scientific Research:** UNCLOS promotes international cooperation in marine scientific research and sets guidelines for the conduct of such research in the EEZ and on the high seas.

13. **Conservation of Marine Living Resources:** The treaty addresses the conservation and sustainable management of marine living resources, including fish stocks.

UNCLOS is a critical framework for managing and protecting the world's oceans and addressing environmental challenges, such as oil and gas spillages. It provides a legal basis for cooperation and the prevention of environmental harm in maritime areas.

- **The Exclusive Economic Zone and Continental Shelf**

The Exclusive Economic Zone (EEZ) and Continental Shelf are two fundamental concepts in the United Nations Convention on the Law of the Sea (UNCLOS), which play a crucial role in the management and governance of marine resources and environments, including addressing issues related to oil and gas spillages. Here's an explanation of each:

Exclusive Economic Zone (EEZ):

1. **Definition:** An EEZ is a maritime zone that extends up to 200 nautical miles (approximately 370 kilometers) from the baselines of a coastal state. In this zone, the coastal state has special rights and jurisdiction over the exploration and exploitation of natural resources, both living and non-living, in the water column and on or under the seabed.

2. **Rights of the Coastal State:**

- **Sovereign Rights:** The coastal state has sovereign rights over all natural resources within its EEZ, including fish, oil, gas, minerals, and other resources. These rights are exclusive, meaning no other state can claim or exercise similar rights within the EEZ.

- **Environmental Protection:** The coastal state is responsible for the protection and preservation of the marine environment within its EEZ. It is obligated to prevent and control pollution and is liable for damage caused by pollution incidents, such as oil spills.

- **Marine Scientific Research:** The coastal state has the authority to regulate and permit marine scientific research in its EEZ.

- **Enforcement of Laws:** The coastal state can enforce its laws and regulations within the EEZ, including those related to resource management and environmental protection.

3. **Freedom of Navigation:** While the coastal state has rights and jurisdiction in the EEZ, other states enjoy the freedom of navigation and overflight in the EEZ, as well as the freedom to lay submarine cables and pipelines.

4. **Beyond 200 Nautical Miles:** If the continental shelf of the coastal state extends beyond 200 nautical miles, it may claim an extended continental shelf, subject to certain criteria and procedures outlined in UNCLOS.

Continental Shelf:

1.   **Definition:** The continental shelf is an extension of a coastal state's land territory and is defined as the seabed and subsoil of the submarine areas that extend beyond the territorial sea, throughout the natural prolongation of the land territory to the outer edge of the continental margin, or up to 200 nautical miles from the baseline if the natural continental margin does not extend that far.

2.   **Rights of the Coastal State:**

•   **Exploration and Exploitation:** The coastal state has sovereign rights over the exploration and exploitation of natural resources on and under the continental shelf, including oil and gas reserves, minerals, and other resources.

•   **Environmental Protection:** The coastal state is responsible for ensuring the protection and preservation of the marine environment on the continental shelf.

3.   **Limits of the Continental Shelf:** The outer limits of the continental shelf are determined based on geological and geophysical criteria. Coastal states can make submissions to the Commission on the Limits of the Continental Shelf, a body established under UNCLOS, to have these limits officially recognized.

4.   **Beyond 200 Nautical Miles:** If the continental shelf extends beyond 200 nautical miles, a coastal state can claim an extended

continental shelf, subject to the criteria and procedures outlined in UNCLOS.

The EEZ and continental shelf concepts are fundamental in providing coastal states with the rights and responsibilities to manage and protect marine resources and environments. They also contribute to international cooperation and shared responsibility in addressing environmental challenges, such as oil and gas spillages, that occur within these maritime zones.

- **The Convention on Biological Diversity and UNCLOS**

The Convention on Biological Diversity (CBD) and the United Nations Convention on the Law of the Sea (UNCLOS) are two international treaties that address different aspects of environmental and marine conservation. Here's how they relate to each other:

1. The Convention on Biological Diversity (CBD):

- **Focus:** The CBD is an international treaty that primarily focuses on the conservation and sustainable use of biodiversity. It is one of the key agreements addressing global biodiversity loss and related issues.

- **Objectives:** The CBD aims to promote the conservation of biological diversity, the sustainable use of its components, and the fair and equitable sharing of benefits arising from genetic resources. It also emphasizes the importance of protecting ecosystems and species.

- **Relevance to Marine Biodiversity:** While the CBD addresses biodiversity in various ecosystems, it has a significant impact on marine biodiversity. Marine ecosystems are rich in biodiversity, and the CBD emphasizes the need to conserve and sustainably manage these resources.

- **Access and Benefit-Sharing (ABS):** The CBD's Nagoya Protocol on ABS is relevant to marine genetic resources. It addresses the fair and equitable sharing of benefits from the utilization of genetic resources, which can include those found in marine environments.

- **Marine Protected Areas (MPAs):** The CBD encourages the establishment of Marine Protected Areas (MPAs) to protect marine biodiversity and ecosystems. It sets targets for the expansion of MPAs to conserve and manage marine resources.

2. The United Nations Convention on the Law of the Sea (UNCLOS):

- **Focus:** UNCLOS is a comprehensive international treaty that primarily deals with issues related to the law of the sea, including maritime boundaries, navigation, resource management, and environmental protection.

- **Objectives:** UNCLOS establishes the legal framework for the use and conservation of the world's oceans and their resources. It addresses issues such as maritime boundaries, the rights and responsibilities of coastal states and other states, the protection of the marine environment, and the sustainable use of marine resources.

- **Relevance to Marine Biodiversity:** UNCLOS is relevant to marine biodiversity conservation in several ways. It establishes provisions for the protection of the marine environment, including the prevention of marine pollution and the conservation of marine living resources.

- **Exclusive Economic Zone (EEZ):** UNCLOS defines the EEZ, where coastal states have special rights and responsibilities over the management of marine resources, including marine biodiversity within their EEZ.

- **High Seas:** UNCLOS addresses the protection and preservation of the marine environment in the high seas, which includes marine biodiversity. It encourages cooperation among states for the conservation and sustainable use of high seas resources.

- **Marine Scientific Research:** UNCLOS provides a framework for marine scientific research, which can contribute to the understanding and conservation of marine biodiversity.

Relation Between CBD and UNCLOS:

The CBD and UNCLOS are interconnected, especially regarding marine biodiversity and the conservation of living marine resources. They complement each other in the following ways:

1. **Cooperative Approach:** Both treaties recognize the need for international cooperation to address marine biodiversity conservation. UNCLOS provides a legal framework for cooperation in the management of marine resources, while the CBD focuses on broader biodiversity conservation goals.

2. **Integrated Conservation:** The two treaties encourage an integrated approach to marine biodiversity conservation, considering both the conservation of ecosystems and the sustainable use of marine resources.

3. **Protection of Marine Ecosystems:** The CBD encourages the conservation of marine ecosystems, which aligns with UNCLOS's emphasis on protecting the marine environment.

4. **Marine Protected Areas:** Both treaties support the establishment of MPAs to protect marine biodiversity, with UNCLOS providing the legal framework for creating and managing these areas.

In summary, the CBD and UNCLOS work together to promote the conservation of marine biodiversity and the sustainable use of marine resources. Their respective provisions and objectives are interrelated, emphasizing the importance of international cooperation and integrated approaches to address marine conservation challenges.

- **State Responsibility and Liability**

"State Responsibility and Liability" is a fundamental concept in international law, particularly within the context of addressing environmental issues such as oil and gas spillages. It outlines the legal obligations of states, their liability for harm caused by their actions, and the principles by which they are held accountable. Here's an overview of state responsibility and liability:

State Responsibility:

1. **Definition:** State responsibility refers to the legal obligations that states have under international law. States are responsible for their conduct, which includes actions or omissions that can result in harm to other states, their citizens, or the global community as a whole.

2. **Basis of State Responsibility:** State responsibility can arise from violations of international treaties, customary international law, or general principles of law recognized by the international community.

3. **Attribution:** State responsibility is attributed to the state for the actions of its government, agencies, or other entities acting on

its behalf. It can also apply to state conduct that occurs beyond its territorial boundaries.

4.   **Elements of State Responsibility:** For state responsibility to be established, several elements must be satisfied, including:

- **Wrongful Act:** The state must commit a wrongful act, which can involve actions that breach international legal obligations, including those related to environmental protection.

- **Attribution:** The wrongful act must be attributable to the state, meaning it is the state's responsibility or that of entities under its control.

- **Damage or Harm:** There must be actual damage, injury, or harm caused by the wrongful act. In the context of oil and gas spillages, this can include environmental damage, economic losses, or harm to other states' interests.

- **Causation:** There must be a causal link between the wrongful act and the resulting harm. The harm must be a direct consequence of the state's actions or omissions.

5.   **Consequences of State Responsibility:** When a state is found responsible for a wrongful act, it may be required to provide remedies, which can include:

- Compensation to the injured party for the harm suffered.

-     Cessation of the wrongful act or preventing its continuation.

-     Reparations or restitution to restore the situation to what it was before the wrongful act occurred.

State Liability:

1. **Definition:** State liability refers to the legal obligation of a state to provide compensation or remedies for the harm or damage caused by its wrongful actions or omissions.

2. **Environmental Liability:** In the context of environmental issues like oil and gas spillages, state liability may arise when a state fails to prevent, respond to, or mitigate environmental harm resulting from activities within its jurisdiction.

3. **Polluter Pays Principle:** The polluter pays principle is a key concept in environmental liability. It holds that those responsible for environmental damage, such as oil spills, should bear the costs of cleanup and compensation to affected parties.

4. **International Environmental Agreements:** Many international environmental agreements, such as the International Convention on Civil Liability for Oil Pollution Damage (CLC) and the International Convention on the Establishment of an International Fund for Compensation for Oil Pollution Damage (FUND), outline state liability and compensation mechanisms for oil pollution incidents.

5. **Shared Responsibility:** In cases where multiple states are involved in an environmental incident, the concept of shared or joint responsibility may apply. States may collectively be held liable for the damage caused.

In the context of oil and gas spillages, state responsibility and liability are essential for ensuring that states take appropriate measures to prevent spills, respond effectively to incidents, and compensate those affected by environmental harm. These principles underscore the importance of holding states accountable for their actions in the international arena and promoting environmental protection.

- **UNCLOS and Dispute Resolution Mechanisms**

The United Nations Convention on the Law of the Sea (UNCLOS) provides a comprehensive legal framework for the governance of the world's oceans and their resources. Dispute resolution mechanisms are a crucial component of UNCLOS, as they help resolve conflicts and disagreements among states concerning the interpretation and application of the convention. Here are some key aspects of UNCLOS dispute resolution mechanisms:

1. **Negotiation:** UNCLOS emphasizes negotiation as the primary means for resolving disputes. Parties to a dispute are encouraged to engage in direct negotiations to find a mutually

acceptable solution. UNCLOS recognizes the importance of peaceful settlement and good-faith negotiations.

2. **Obligation to Exchange Information:** UNCLOS requires the parties involved in a dispute to exchange relevant information and data to facilitate informed negotiations. Transparency and openness are fundamental to the negotiation process.

3. **Third-Party Dispute Settlement:** When direct negotiations fail to resolve a dispute, UNCLOS provides several options for third-party dispute settlement. These mechanisms include:

a. **International Tribunal for the Law of the Sea (ITLOS):** ITLOS is an independent judicial body established by UNCLOS to adjudicate disputes related to the interpretation and application of the convention. It hears cases brought by states and provides binding decisions.

b. **International Court of Justice (ICJ):** States may choose to bring their disputes before the ICJ, a principal judicial organ of the United Nations. While the ICJ does not exclusively deal with UNCLOS-related cases, it has jurisdiction over cases that involve the interpretation and application of the convention.

c. **Arbitration:** Parties to a dispute may opt for arbitration to resolve their differences. UNCLOS provides detailed rules and procedures for arbitration, and the resulting awards are binding on the parties.

4.   **Specialized Annexes:** UNCLOS includes specific dispute resolution mechanisms for certain types of disputes. For example, Annex VII of UNCLOS deals with the settlement of disputes concerning the interpretation or application of the convention related to particular subject matters, such as fisheries or the protection and preservation of the marine environment.

5.   **Optional Treaties:** States may also choose to settle disputes through specialized agreements and treaties. For instance, some states have established regional fisheries agreements to resolve issues related to shared fish stocks and prevent overfishing.

6.   **Prompt Release of Vessels:** UNCLOS includes provisions related to the prompt release of vessels and crews detained for violations in a foreign state's territorial waters or exclusive economic zone. These provisions help prevent prolonged detentions and potential disputes.

7.   **Compliance and Enforcement:** UNCLOS also includes mechanisms for enforcing decisions and ensuring compliance with the convention's provisions. States are expected to abide by and implement decisions reached through dispute resolution mechanisms.

8.   **Amicable Settlement:** UNCLOS encourages parties to seek amicable solutions whenever possible, even during the course of formal dispute resolution proceedings. Amicable settlement can involve mediation or other peaceful means to resolve the dispute.

UNCLOS's dispute resolution mechanisms play a critical role in maintaining peace and stability in the world's oceans. By providing clear processes for resolving conflicts related to maritime boundaries, resource exploitation, environmental protection, and other issues, UNCLOS contributes to the peaceful coexistence of states and the sustainable management of the marine environment.

CHAPTER 4
INTERNATIONAL ENVIRONMENTAL AGREEMENTS

- **The MARPOL Convention**

The MARPOL Convention, short for the International Convention for the Prevention of Pollution from Ships (MARPOL), is a significant international treaty aimed at preventing and controlling various forms of marine pollution caused by ships. Here are the key aspects of the MARPOL Convention:

1. **Objective:** The primary objective of MARPOL is to reduce and ultimately eliminate pollution from ships that poses threats to the marine environment and human health. It covers various types of pollution, including oil, chemicals, sewage, garbage, and air emissions.

2. **Annexes:** MARPOL is organized into six annexes, each addressing specific types of pollution. These annexes are as follows:

- Annex I: Prevention of Pollution by Oil (oil pollution).

- Annex II: Control of Pollution by Noxious Liquid Substances in Bulk (chemical pollution).

- Annex III: Prevention of Pollution by Harmful Substances Carried by Sea in Packaged Form (hazardous substances in packaged form).

- Annex IV: Prevention of Pollution by Sewage from Ships (sewage pollution).

- Annex V: Prevention of Pollution by Garbage from Ships (garbage pollution).

- Annex VI: Prevention of Air Pollution from Ships (air emissions).

3. **Regulations and Requirements:** Each annex of MARPOL sets out specific regulations, requirements, and limitations related to the prevention and control of pollution from ships. These regulations vary depending on the type of pollution and the nature of the substances involved.

4. **Pollution Prevention Measures:** MARPOL includes a wide range of measures for preventing pollution, such as oil discharge standards, limits on emissions of air pollutants, rules for the discharge of sewage and garbage, and guidelines for handling hazardous materials. It also establishes prohibited zones for the disposal of waste materials at sea.

5. **International Standards:** MARPOL sets international standards for the design, construction, and operation of ships to minimize their environmental impact. For example, it includes

guidelines for the design of oil tankers and bulk carriers to reduce the risk of oil spills.

6. **Special Areas:** The convention designates Special Areas with stringent pollution control measures, such as the Baltic Sea and the North Sea. In these areas, additional regulations and stricter controls are in place to protect sensitive ecosystems.

7. **Port State Control:** MARPOL enables port state authorities to inspect ships for compliance with the convention's requirements. Ships found to be in violation may be detained, fined, or prohibited from entering certain ports.

8. **Safeguard Measures:** MARPOL includes provisions for the establishment of reception facilities for the disposal of ship-generated waste and residue. These facilities ensure that ships have adequate means to offload waste materials at ports.

9. **Amendments and Updates:** The MARPOL Convention is periodically updated and amended to address emerging environmental challenges and technological advancements. These updates ensure that the convention remains relevant and effective.

10. **Global Adoption:** MARPOL is one of the most widely adopted conventions in international maritime law. It is enforced by many countries, including coastal states, flag states, and port states, making it a significant tool for the protection of the marine environment.

MARPOL is a crucial instrument for the prevention of pollution from ships and plays a vital role in the protection of the world's oceans and marine ecosystems. It reflects the international community's commitment to reducing the environmental impact of maritime activities and promoting sustainable shipping practices.

- **The OSPAR Convention**

The OSPAR Convention, officially known as the "Convention for the Protection of the Marine Environment of the North-East Atlantic," is a regional treaty that aims to protect and conserve the marine environment of the North-East Atlantic. It was adopted in 1992 and is named after the OSPAR Commission, the governing body responsible for implementing and enforcing the convention. Here are the key aspects of the OSPAR Convention:

1. Geographic Scope: The OSPAR Convention covers the marine environment of the North-East Atlantic, which includes the coastal and offshore areas of the North-East Atlantic Ocean, the Arctic and sub-Arctic waters of the Northeast Atlantic, and the associated seabed and subsoil.

2. Environmental Objectives: OSPAR's main objectives are to prevent and eliminate pollution, protect the marine ecosystem, conserve biodiversity, and promote sustainable use of the North-East Atlantic marine environment. It sets specific targets for the protection and preservation of various habitats and species.

3. Annexes: The convention is organized into annexes, each addressing specific issues or types of pollution. Key annexes include:

- **Annex I:** Substances that are considered to be the most dangerous and are subject to restrictions and bans.

- **Annex II:** Hazardous substances and preparation for response to pollution incidents.

- **Annex III:** Coordinated environmental monitoring and assessment.

- **Annex IV:** Oil discharges from offshore platforms.

- **Annex V:** Land-based sources of marine pollution.

- **Annex VI:** Radioactive substances.

- **Annex VII:** Dumping of wastes and other matters.

- **Annex VIII:** Offshore industries.

4. Pollution Prevention and Reduction: OSPAR sets strict limits on the discharge of hazardous substances, including oil and radioactive materials, and regulates the disposal of waste at sea. It promotes the use of best available techniques to minimize pollution from land-based sources and offshore activities.

5. Marine Protected Areas (MPAs): OSPAR designates and manages marine protected areas in the North-East Atlantic to protect vulnerable ecosystems, habitats, and species. These MPAs are essential for conserving biodiversity and promoting sustainable fishing practices.

6. Coordinated Monitoring and Assessment: OSPAR requires member states to cooperate in monitoring and assessing the state of the marine environment. The results of these assessments help inform management and conservation measures.

7. Special Protection Areas (SPAs): OSPAR identifies and protects areas of particular ecological significance, including habitats used by migratory species, through the designation of Special Protection Areas.

8. Emergency Response: OSPAR establishes measures for preparing and responding to pollution incidents, including oil spills and chemical accidents. Member states are required to maintain response capabilities and cooperate during emergencies.

9. Public Participation: OSPAR promotes public participation and transparency in environmental decision-making. It encourages engagement with stakeholders, including NGOs and the public, to ensure that diverse perspectives are considered.

10. Amendments and Reviews: OSPAR is periodically reviewed and amended to adapt to new scientific knowledge and emerging environmental challenges. It ensures the convention remains effective in addressing evolving threats to the North-East Atlantic marine environment.

The OSPAR Convention is a vital instrument for the protection of the marine environment in the North-East Atlantic. It reflects the commitment of its member states to sustainable marine management and the conservation of marine biodiversity in this ecologically significant region.

- **The Arctic Council and the Protection of the Arctic Environment**

The Arctic Council is an intergovernmental forum that plays a crucial role in addressing environmental protection and sustainable development in the Arctic region. It focuses on various aspects of the Arctic environment, including the conservation and protection of the region's fragile ecosystems. Here are key points related to the Arctic Council's role in the protection of the Arctic environment:

1. The Arctic Council: The Arctic Council is an international organization composed of eight Arctic states: Canada, Denmark (representing Greenland and the Faroe Islands), Finland, Iceland, Norway, Russia, Sweden, and the United States. It also includes six permanent participant organizations representing the indigenous peoples of the Arctic.

2. Environmental Protection Mandate: One of the main tasks of the Arctic Council is to address environmental protection in the Arctic region. This includes the conservation of Arctic biodiversity, the prevention of pollution, and the promotion of sustainable development.

3. The Arctic Environmental Protection Strategy (AEPS): The AEPS is a framework adopted by the Arctic Council to guide its work on environmental protection. It encompasses various initiatives aimed at safeguarding the Arctic environment and promoting sustainable practices.

4. Working Groups: The Arctic Council operates through several working groups, each with a specific focus on environmental issues. Some of the key working groups include the Arctic Monitoring and Assessment Programme (AMAP) and the Protection of the Arctic Marine Environment (PAME) working group. These groups conduct assessments, research, and policy development related to environmental protection.

5. Scientific Research: The Arctic Council facilitates scientific research and monitoring to better understand environmental changes in the Arctic, including the impacts of climate change. This research informs policy decisions and environmental protection efforts.

6. Pollution Prevention: The Arctic Council addresses various forms of pollution, including oil spills, chemical contaminants, and waste management, with the aim of preventing environmental harm and protecting Arctic ecosystems.

7. Conservation of Biodiversity: Conservation of Arctic biodiversity, including both terrestrial and marine species, is a priority for the Arctic Council. Efforts are made to protect critical habitats and ensure the sustainability of wildlife populations.

8. Climate Change Mitigation and Adaptation: The Arctic Council recognizes the importance of addressing climate change in the region. This includes efforts to reduce greenhouse gas emissions and to develop strategies for adapting to the environmental changes brought about by a warming Arctic.

9. Indigenous Involvement: The Arctic Council values the involvement of indigenous peoples and their traditional knowledge in environmental protection efforts. Their insights are integral to understanding the environmental challenges and developing effective solutions.

10. Regional Agreements: The Arctic Council has played a role in the negotiation of regional agreements that address environmental protection, such as the Agreement on Cooperation on Aeronautical and Maritime Search and Rescue in the Arctic.

11. International Cooperation: The Arctic Council fosters international cooperation on environmental issues, involving not only the Arctic states but also observer states and organizations that contribute to Arctic governance and environmental protection.

The Arctic Council is an essential platform for addressing the complex and interconnected environmental challenges facing the Arctic region. Its work contributes to the preservation of the unique

Arctic environment, the well-being of indigenous communities, and the sustainable development of the Arctic for future generations.

- **The Role of the Basel Convention**

The Basel Convention on the Control of Transboundary Movements of Hazardous Wastes and Their Disposal is an international treaty that plays a crucial role in regulating the cross-border transport and disposal of hazardous wastes. Here are the key aspects of the Basel Convention's role:

1. **Control of Transboundary Movements:** The primary purpose of the Basel Convention is to regulate the transboundary movement of hazardous wastes. It aims to ensure that the generation, transportation, and disposal of hazardous wastes do not pose environmental or health risks to other countries or regions.

2. **Scope of Application:** The Basel Convention applies to hazardous and other wastes that are intended for transboundary movement. It covers a wide range of materials and substances, including industrial, household, and medical wastes, as well as other types of hazardous waste.

3. **Prior Informed Consent (PIC) Procedure:** The convention establishes a system known as the Prior Informed Consent (PIC) procedure, which requires countries to obtain the informed consent of the receiving country before exporting hazardous wastes. This process ensures that receiving countries

have the capacity and infrastructure to manage and dispose of the waste safely.

4. **Reduction of Hazardous Waste Generation:** The Basel Convention encourages waste minimization and the reduction of hazardous waste generation at the source. It promotes cleaner production practices and the use of environmentally sound technologies.

5. **Environmentally Sound Management:** The convention emphasizes the need for environmentally sound management (ESM) of hazardous wastes. This includes safe handling, storage, and disposal of such waste to prevent environmental contamination and health risks.

6. **Prohibition of Dumping:** The Basel Convention prohibits the dumping of hazardous wastes at sea and on land. This prohibition aims to prevent the disposal of waste in a manner that can harm the environment and human health.

7. **Promotion of Recycling and Recovery:** The convention encourages the recycling and recovery of hazardous waste materials when it can be done safely and in an environmentally sound manner. This reduces the demand for new resources and minimizes the environmental impact of waste disposal.

8. **Technical Assistance and Capacity Building:** The Basel Convention provides support to developing countries and countries

with economies in transition to improve their capacity to manage hazardous wastes. This includes technology transfer, financial assistance, and training programs.

9. **Transparency and Reporting:** Parties to the convention are required to provide information on their hazardous waste generation, management, and movements. This transparency helps monitor compliance and identify areas for improvement.

10. **Parties and Non-Parties:** While the Basel Convention has a significant number of parties, it also acknowledges that not all countries may be able to immediately adhere to its requirements. Therefore, it encourages the responsible management of hazardous wastes even in non-party states and seeks to promote their eventual accession to the convention.

The Basel Convention plays a critical role in addressing the global issue of hazardous waste management and reducing the risk of environmental and health problems associated with the improper handling and disposal of such waste. It underscores the importance of international cooperation and responsible waste management practices to protect the environment and public health.

- **The Aarhus Convention and Public Participation in Environmental Decision-Making**

The Aarhus Convention, officially known as the "Convention on Access to Information, Public Participation in Decision-making and

Access to Justice in Environmental Matters," is a legally binding international treaty that promotes public participation in environmental decision-making, access to information, and access to justice in environmental matters. Here's an overview of the Aarhus Convention and its role in enhancing public participation in environmental issues:

1. Access to Information:

- **Public Right to Access Information:** The Aarhus Convention recognizes the fundamental right of the public to access environmental information held by public authorities. This includes data, documents, and reports related to the environment.

- **Transparency Requirements:** The convention establishes requirements for governments to proactively disseminate environmental information, make it easily accessible to the public, and respond to requests for information in a timely manner.

- **Environmental Information:** Environmental information covers a wide range of topics, including emissions, pollutants, waste management, biodiversity, and the state of the environment. This transparency empowers the public to make informed decisions and participate effectively in environmental matters.

2. Public Participation in Decision-Making:

- **Participation in Environmental Decision-Making:** The Aarhus Convention ensures that the public has the opportunity to participate in decisions that may affect the environment, such as policies, plans, programs, or projects.

- **Early and Effective Participation:** Public participation is encouraged at all stages of the decision-making process, including during the planning, development, and implementation of projects or policies. This early involvement allows the public's concerns and suggestions to be considered.

- **Consultation and Public Access:** Authorities are required to facilitate consultations and provide access to relevant information, as well as involve the public in environmental assessments, permitting processes, and other relevant procedures.

- **Aarhus Convention Compliance Committees:** The convention establishes compliance committees to review cases of non-compliance and ensure that the public's right to participate is upheld.

3. Access to Justice:

- **Access to Justice in Environmental Matters:** The Aarhus Convention provides mechanisms for the public to access justice in environmental matters. This allows individuals and organizations to challenge public decisions that are in violation of environmental laws or that fail to uphold public participation rights.

- **Access to Legal Remedies:** The convention guarantees access to legal remedies and procedures, ensuring that individuals or groups can challenge decisions that negatively impact the environment.

- **Financial Barriers:** To facilitate access to justice, the Aarhus Convention may provide for mechanisms to reduce financial barriers that could prevent individuals and organizations from pursuing environmental cases.

4. Public Participation in International Forums:

- The Aarhus Convention recognizes the importance of public participation in international environmental forums. It encourages governments to ensure the public's voice is heard in transboundary or international environmental matters.

- This provision extends the principles of public participation to global environmental governance and decision-making.

The Aarhus Convention empowers the public by granting them access to environmental information, facilitating active participation in environmental decision-making processes, and providing access to justice when environmental laws and regulations are not upheld. It promotes accountability and transparency in environmental governance, ultimately contributing to better environmental protection and sustainable development.

CHAPTER 5

STATE RESPONSIBILITY AND LIABILITY

- **Proving State Responsibility**

Proving state responsibility in international law involves establishing that a state has violated its obligations under international treaties, customary international law, or other recognized principles, and that it should be held accountable for its actions. Proving state responsibility is a complex process that typically requires a combination of legal, factual, and evidentiary elements. Here are the key steps and considerations in proving state responsibility:

1. Identify the Legal Basis: The first step in proving state responsibility is to identify the legal obligations that the state is alleged to have violated. This could involve international treaties, customary international law, or general principles of law.

2. Establish the Violation: To prove state responsibility, you must demonstrate that the state has committed a wrongful act, which could involve actions or omissions that breach its international legal obligations. This may include causing harm to another state, its citizens, or the global community.

3. Show Attribution: It is essential to establish that the wrongful act is attributable to the state. This can involve showing that the state's government, agencies, or other entities were responsible for the act, whether directly or indirectly.

4. Prove Damage or Harm: To demonstrate state responsibility, you must show that actual harm or damage resulted from the wrongful act. This can include environmental damage, economic losses, or harm to the rights of other states or individuals.

5. Causation: You need to establish a causal link between the wrongful act and the resulting harm. It should be clear that the harm is a direct consequence of the state's actions or omissions.

6. Document Evidence: The process of proving state responsibility often involves collecting and presenting evidence to support your case. This may include documents, witness testimonies, expert reports, and other forms of evidence.

7. Legal Arguments: Legal arguments and interpretations of relevant international law must be presented to demonstrate that the state's actions or omissions violated specific legal obligations.

8. Counterarguments: Expect that the accused state may present counterarguments and evidence to defend itself. As part of the legal process, you will need to address these counterarguments.

9. Legal Proceedings: Proving state responsibility can involve legal proceedings at the international level. This may include presenting your case before international courts or tribunals, such as the International Court of Justice (ICJ) or specialized tribunals.

10. Remedies: If state responsibility is established, remedies may be sought. These could include compensation for the harm caused, cessation of the wrongful act, or other measures to restore the situation to what it was before the wrongful act occurred.

11. Enforcement: Even when state responsibility is proven and remedies are granted, enforcing those remedies can be challenging. International enforcement mechanisms may be required to ensure compliance.

Proving state responsibility is a complex legal process that requires a strong foundation in international law and a thorough understanding of the specific case at hand. It often involves legal expertise, expert witnesses, and the coordination of resources to present a compelling case before international bodies or tribunals.

- **Compensation Mechanisms**

Compensation mechanisms in international law are designed to provide remedies to individuals, entities, or states that have suffered harm or damages due to the actions of another state or entity. These mechanisms are essential for addressing and rectifying violations of international law and ensuring accountability. Here are some key compensation mechanisms in international law:

1. State-to-State Compensation:

- In many cases, disputes between states are resolved through diplomatic negotiations or the use of dispute settlement mechanisms, such as arbitration or adjudication. As part of the resolution process, states may agree to provide compensation to the injured state for harm caused by a wrongful act.

- The compensation may take various forms, including monetary payments, restitution, or specific performance to remedy the harm or damage.

2. International Courts and Tribunals:

- International courts and tribunals, such as the International Court of Justice (ICJ), hear cases involving state responsibility and may order compensation as part of their judgments. States that are parties to such courts are legally bound to comply with their decisions.

- For example, the ICJ has ruled on numerous cases involving state responsibility and compensation, including cases related to violations of international treaties, boundary disputes, and environmental harm.

3. Claims Commissions:

- In some cases, states establish claims commissions or special arbitral bodies to adjudicate and settle claims for compensation. These commissions are often used to resolve historical disputes or conflicts.

- The Iran-United States Claims Tribunal, established in the aftermath of the Iranian Revolution, is an example of a claims commission that handled a large number of compensation claims.

4. International Environmental Agreements:

- Various international environmental agreements, such as the Convention on Civil Liability for Oil Pollution Damage (CLC) and the International Convention on the Establishment of an International Fund for Compensation for Oil Pollution Damage (FUND), provide compensation mechanisms for damage caused by oil spills.

- These agreements establish funds to compensate victims of oil pollution incidents, and the compensation is typically funded by contributions from the shipping industry.

5. International Human Rights Bodies:

- International human rights bodies, such as the European Court of Human Rights and the Inter-American Court of Human Rights, may order compensation for individuals or groups who have been victims of human rights violations.

- Compensation can include monetary awards, rehabilitation, and restitution for victims.

6. Investment Arbitration:

• Investment treaties often include mechanisms for investor-state arbitration. When a foreign investor believes its investments have been expropriated or otherwise harmed by a host state's actions, it can bring a claim for compensation.

• Arbitral tribunals, established under investment treaties, may award monetary compensation to the investor for the losses suffered.

7. Environmental Liability and Polluter Pays Principles:

• In the context of environmental harm, the "polluter pays" principle holds that those responsible for environmental damage should bear the costs of cleanup and compensation.

• Domestic and international environmental laws often incorporate this principle, and compensation mechanisms may include fines and penalties imposed on polluters to fund environmental remediation and compensate affected parties.

Compensation mechanisms in international law serve to restore the injured party to the position it would have been in had the wrongful act not occurred. These mechanisms play a crucial role in upholding the rule of law, ensuring accountability, and promoting the peaceful resolution of disputes between states and the protection of individuals and the environment.

- **Jurisdictional Issues and Remedies**

Jurisdictional issues and remedies are central to the field of international law, governing how states and international organizations can exercise authority and address violations of international law. Here are key aspects of jurisdictional issues and the remedies available in international law:

Jurisdictional Issues:

1. **Territorial Jurisdiction:** This refers to a state's authority over activities and events occurring within its territory. States have primary jurisdiction to enforce and apply their laws within their borders. Territorial jurisdiction is a fundamental principle of international law.

2. **Extraterritorial Jurisdiction:** In some cases, states may extend their jurisdiction beyond their borders. Extraterritorial jurisdiction can be based on various factors, including the nationality principle (jurisdiction over their own citizens' actions abroad), the protective principle (jurisdiction to protect the state's essential interests), and the passive personality principle (jurisdiction over crimes committed against their citizens abroad).

3. **Subjective Jurisdiction:** This pertains to a state's authority over its own citizens or entities, allowing the state to regulate their conduct and, if necessary, exercise jurisdiction over them for violations committed abroad.

4.   **Universal Jurisdiction:** Universal jurisdiction allows states to prosecute and punish certain international crimes, such as war crimes, crimes against humanity, and genocide, regardless of the location of the crime or the nationality of the perpetrator or victim. Universal jurisdiction is typically based on the idea that certain crimes are of universal concern and should not go unpunished.

5.   **Jurisdictional Immunities:** States generally enjoy immunity from the jurisdiction of foreign courts. However, this immunity is not absolute, and exceptions exist, especially in cases involving commercial activities or gross violations of human rights. International organizations may also have jurisdictional immunities, subject to certain limitations.

Remedies:

1.   **Diplomatic Resolution:** When disputes between states arise, diplomatic means of dispute settlement are often the first option. Diplomatic remedies include negotiations, consultations, and mediation with the aim of reaching a mutually acceptable solution.

2.   **Arbitration:** States may agree to submit a dispute to arbitration, either on an ad hoc basis or through permanent arbitration institutions. Arbitration provides a binding resolution through the decision of an independent tribunal.

3. **Judicial Remedies:** International courts and tribunals, such as the International Court of Justice (ICJ) or regional human rights courts, offer judicial remedies. These bodies can issue judgments and advisory opinions on issues brought before them.

4. **Compensation:** Monetary compensation is a common remedy for violations of international law, especially when the wrongful act results in financial losses or damage. Compensation can be awarded by international tribunals, claims commissions, or through state-to-state negotiations.

5. **Injunctions and Orders:** In certain situations, international courts may issue orders or injunctions to prevent ongoing or potential harm. These orders can include measures to protect the environment, prohibit certain activities, or safeguard the rights of individuals or states.

6. **Restitution:** Restitution involves restoring the situation to what it was before the wrongful act occurred. It may be ordered to remedy violations of international law, such as the unlawful expropriation of property.

7. **Satisfaction and Apology:** International law may require a responsible state to offer satisfaction to the injured state or individual, which can include an official apology or acknowledgment of the wrong committed.

8. **Non-Recognition and Countermeasures:** States may choose not to recognize certain actions taken by other states in violation of international law. They can also take countermeasures to respond to violations and induce compliance.

9. **Sanctions:** In some cases, states may impose sanctions, such as economic or trade measures, to encourage a state to comply with international law. Sanctions can serve as a form of remedy and a means of influencing state behavior.

Jurisdictional issues and remedies in international law are complex and diverse, reflecting the evolving nature of international relations and the need to address violations of international norms and obligations. The choice of remedy depends on the specific circumstances of each case and the mechanisms available under relevant international agreements and laws.

- **Case Studies of State Responsibility**

Understanding state responsibility in the context of international law often requires examining real-world case studies to illustrate how it is applied in practice. Here are three case studies of state responsibility:

1. **The Trail Smelter Dispute (United States and Canada):**

- In the early 20th century, the Trail Smelter, located in British Columbia, Canada, released significant amounts of air pollution containing sulfur dioxide into the atmosphere. This pollution traveled across the border into the state of Washington, United States, causing damage to agricultural crops and forests.

•	The United States brought the case before an arbitral tribunal, which found that Canada was responsible for the transboundary harm caused by the smelter. The tribunal ruled that Canada was in violation of international law by allowing the pollution to cross the border and held that it was responsible for the damage to U.S. territory.

•	This case is notable as an early example of state responsibility for transboundary environmental harm and established the principle that states are responsible for preventing harm to neighboring states caused by activities within their borders.

2.	**The Case of Nicaragua v. United States (International Court of Justice):**

•	This case, brought before the International Court of Justice (ICJ) in the 1980s, concerned the United States' support for armed activities in Nicaragua. Nicaragua claimed that the United States had violated international law by providing military and financial assistance to rebel groups (the Contras) in Nicaragua.

•	The ICJ, in its 1986 judgment, found the United States responsible for violating Nicaragua's sovereignty and engaging in unlawful use of force. The court ordered the United States to pay reparations to Nicaragua.

• This case illustrates state responsibility in the context of non-intervention and the prohibition on the use of force under international law.

3. **The Chorzów Factory Case (Poland v. Germany, Permanent Court of International Justice):**

• The Chorzów Factory case, decided by the Permanent Court of International Justice (the predecessor to the ICJ) in 1928, concerned damage caused to a German-owned factory located in the Polish town of Chorzów.

• The court held that Poland had violated international law by expropriating the factory without adequate compensation. The judgment ordered Poland to pay reparations to Germany.

• This case is an early example of state responsibility for unlawful expropriation under international law, establishing principles for the protection of foreign property rights.

These case studies highlight various aspects of state responsibility in international law, including the responsibility for transboundary harm, violations of sovereignty, and unlawful use of force. They demonstrate how international tribunals, including the ICJ, play a role in determining and enforcing state responsibility, often resulting in compensation or other remedies for the injured party.

- **The Role of International Courts and Tribunals**

International courts and tribunals play a crucial role in the international legal system by resolving disputes between states, individuals, and international organizations. They help uphold and interpret international law, provide legal remedies, and promote the peaceful resolution of conflicts. Here's an overview of the role of international courts and tribunals:

1. **Conflict Resolution:** International courts and tribunals serve as mechanisms for resolving conflicts and disputes among states, international organizations, and sometimes individuals. They provide a peaceful and lawful alternative to the use of force.

2. **Interpretation of International Law:** International courts and tribunals interpret and clarify the principles and rules of international law. Their decisions serve as precedents, guiding state behavior and legal practice in international relations.

3. **Adjudication of Disputes:** These institutions adjudicate disputes across a wide range of areas, including territorial disputes, human rights violations, trade issues, environmental concerns, and treaty interpretation. For example, the International Court of Justice (ICJ) settles legal disputes between states.

4. **Enforcement of International Law:** The decisions of international courts and tribunals are generally binding on the

parties involved. States are expected to comply with judgments and rulings, and non-compliance can result in international sanctions.

5. **Protection of Human Rights:** Human rights courts and tribunals, such as the European Court of Human Rights and the Inter-American Court of Human Rights, address human rights violations and provide remedies for individuals whose rights have been infringed upon by states.

6. **Arbitration and Mediation:** International arbitration and mediation tribunals offer methods of alternative dispute resolution. They help parties negotiate settlements and resolve disputes without resorting to litigation in traditional courts.

7. **Preventive Diplomacy:** Some international courts and tribunals, like the Permanent Court of Arbitration, engage in preventive diplomacy by facilitating discussions and negotiations between states to avoid conflicts.

8. **Implementation of Treaty Obligations:** Courts and tribunals ensure that states fulfill their treaty obligations. They can assess whether states have violated their commitments under international agreements and, if necessary, issue judgments and sanctions.

9. **Environmental Protection:** Environmental courts and tribunals, such as the World Trade Organization's (WTO) dispute

settlement system, address trade-related environmental issues. They help ensure that trade practices do not harm the environment.

10. **Resolution of Investment Disputes:** Investment arbitration tribunals, often established under bilateral or multilateral investment treaties, handle disputes between states and foreign investors. They can award damages and compensation for investors when states violate their treaty obligations.

11. **Promotion of Legal Certainty:** International courts and tribunals contribute to the development and clarification of international law, which in turn enhances legal certainty in international relations.

12. **Deterrence of Wrongful Behavior:** The existence of international courts and tribunals can deter states from engaging in wrongful behavior, as they are aware that they may be held accountable for their actions.

13. **Expertise and Independence:** These institutions consist of expert judges and arbitrators who possess a deep understanding of international law. Their impartiality and independence are essential for ensuring fair and just outcomes.

International courts and tribunals are integral to the rule-based international system, providing mechanisms for addressing disputes, upholding the principles of international law, and advancing the cause of peace, justice, and cooperation in the international community. They promote a world in which conflicts can be resolved through legal processes rather than through force and coercion.

CHAPTER 6
PREVENTION AND PREPAREDNESS

- **Early Warning Systems**

Early warning systems are crucial tools in disaster management and conflict prevention, designed to detect and provide advance notice of potential threats or hazards. These systems serve to reduce risks, minimize the impact of disasters, and save lives. Early warning systems are applied in various contexts, including natural disasters, public health emergencies, and conflicts. Here's an overview of early warning systems and their significance:

1. **Natural Disasters:**

- **Earthquakes:** Seismometers and seismic networks detect ground motion and provide early warning of impending earthquakes. Alerts can be issued to the public, allowing people to seek shelter.

- **Tsunamis:** Oceanographic sensors and buoys in the sea detect tsunami waves, triggering alerts to coastal communities.

- **Floods:** Hydrological monitoring and weather forecasting systems track rainfall, river levels, and weather patterns to predict and warn of potential floods.

- **Wildfires:** Remote sensing technology and weather data help predict and monitor wildfire behavior, allowing for timely evacuation orders and firefighting efforts.

2. **Public Health Emergencies:**

- **Pandemics:** Disease surveillance systems monitor the spread of diseases and detect potential outbreaks. Alerts and advisories are issued to health authorities and the public.

- **Biological and Chemical Threats:** Early warning systems track unusual patterns of illness or the release of harmful substances, helping to identify and respond to biological or chemical threats.

3. **Conflict Prevention and Security:**

- **Conflict Early Warning Systems:** These systems collect data on factors that may lead to conflicts, such as political tensions, social unrest, and human rights abuses. By analyzing this data, early warning systems aim to predict and prevent conflicts or atrocities.

- **Security Threats:** Security forces and intelligence agencies use early warning systems to detect and counteract threats, such as terrorism, cyberattacks, and unconventional warfare.

4. **Environmental Monitoring:**

- **Air Quality and Pollution:** Environmental monitoring systems track air quality, water quality, and pollution levels. Warnings are issued when pollutant levels exceed safe thresholds.

- **Climate Change and Extreme Weather:** Climate monitoring systems track changes in climate patterns and provide forecasts for extreme weather events, such as hurricanes, droughts, and heatwaves.

5. **Humanitarian Crises:**

- **Food Security:** Early warning systems for food security use data on crop production, food prices, and other factors to predict food shortages and famine.

- **Displacement and Refugee Movements:** Monitoring systems track population movements and alert governments and humanitarian organizations to the potential for refugee crises.

6. **Communication and Alert Systems:**

- Early warning systems rely on various communication channels, including mobile phone networks, radio, television, sirens, and social media, to disseminate alerts and information to the affected population.

- Mobile apps and text messages are increasingly used to provide timely warnings and instructions to individuals.

7. Community Preparedness:

- Early warning systems are most effective when combined with community preparedness and response plans. Communities are educated on how to react to alerts and are trained in evacuation and safety measures.

Early warning systems are a vital component of disaster risk reduction and response efforts. Their effectiveness depends on the accuracy and timeliness of data, the availability of infrastructure and resources, and the capacity of governments and organizations to respond to warnings. These systems not only save lives but also contribute to overall resilience and preparedness in the face of various threats and hazards.

• Contingency Planning

Contingency planning is a systematic process of developing strategies and action plans to address and respond to potential risks, emergencies, or unexpected events. These plans are essential for organizations, governments, and individuals to ensure preparedness and mitigate the impact of unforeseen circumstances. Contingency planning involves the following key steps:

1. **Risk Assessment:**

•   Identify potential risks and hazards that could disrupt normal operations or cause harm. These risks can include natural disasters, pandemics, economic downturns, security breaches, or technological failures.

2. **Prioritization:**

•   Prioritize risks based on their likelihood and potential impact. Determine which risks require immediate attention and allocate resources accordingly.

3. **Setting Objectives:**

•   Define clear and achievable objectives for the contingency plan. Establish what needs to be protected, recovered, or maintained during and after a crisis.

4. **Resource Allocation:**

•   Allocate the necessary resources, including personnel, equipment, financial reserves, and technology, to implement the contingency plan effectively.

5. **Plan Development:**

•   Develop specific action plans and procedures for responding to each identified risk. These plans should outline roles and responsibilities, communication strategies, and the steps to be taken in case of an emergency.

6. **Communication Plan:**

- Establish a clear communication plan that includes internal and external stakeholders. Ensure that all parties involved are aware of their roles and responsibilities during a crisis.

7. **Testing and Training:**

- Regularly conduct drills, exercises, and training sessions to familiarize staff with the contingency plan. Testing helps identify weaknesses and areas for improvement.

8. **Data Backup and Recovery:**

- Implement data backup and recovery strategies to safeguard critical information. Ensure that data can be restored quickly in case of data loss or system failures.

9. **Security Measures:**

- Enhance security measures to protect assets and sensitive information. This includes measures to prevent cyberattacks, unauthorized access, or physical breaches.

10. **Financial Contingency:**

- Establish financial reserves or lines of credit to cover unexpected expenses that may arise during a crisis. Develop strategies to maintain financial stability.

11. **Supply Chain Management:**

- Evaluate and diversify supply chains to reduce dependence on single suppliers. This can help ensure a continuous flow of goods and services during disruptions.

12. **Emergency Response:**

- Develop emergency response plans, including evacuation procedures, first aid, and safety protocols, to protect the health and well-being of employees and the public.

13. **Documentation:**

- Maintain comprehensive documentation of the contingency plan, including contact information, procedures, and important records. Ensure that the documentation is easily accessible during a crisis.

14. **Review and Revision:**

- Continuously review and update the contingency plan to account for changing risks, evolving business processes, and lessons learned from past incidents.

15. **Crisis Management Team:**

- Designate a crisis management team with clearly defined roles and responsibilities. This team is responsible for making critical decisions during a crisis.

Contingency planning is an ongoing process that requires adaptability and a commitment to preparedness. The goal is to minimize disruption, protect lives and assets, and facilitate a rapid recovery when unforeseen events occur. Organizations and individuals that invest time and resources in contingency planning are better equipped to respond effectively to emergencies and challenges.

- **International Best Practices in Spill Prevention**

International best practices in spill prevention are crucial for safeguarding the environment, public health, and economic well-being. They provide a framework for industries, governments, and organizations to minimize the risk of oil and gas spillages and ensure effective response measures are in place. Here are some key international best practices in spill prevention:

1. **Comprehensive Regulatory Frameworks:**

- Develop and enforce comprehensive regulatory frameworks that set standards for spill prevention, preparedness, and response. These regulations should apply to all relevant industries, including oil and gas exploration, shipping, and transportation.

2. **Risk Assessment and Management:**

- Conduct thorough risk assessments to identify potential spill risks and vulnerabilities. Implement risk management plans to reduce the likelihood and impact of spills.

3. **Safety Standards and Practices:**

- Adhere to internationally recognized safety standards, such as those provided by organizations like the International Maritime Organization (IMO) and the International Association of Oil & Gas Producers (IOGP). These standards cover vessel design, equipment maintenance, and operational practices.

4. **Technology and Innovation:**

- Embrace technological advancements to enhance spill prevention. This includes using state-of-the-art equipment, such as double-hulled tankers, blowout preventers, and advanced monitoring systems.

5. **Training and Education:**

- Provide comprehensive training and education to personnel involved in oil and gas operations. Ensure they are well-informed about safety protocols, emergency response procedures, and environmental risks.

6. **Environmental Impact Assessments:**

- Conduct thorough environmental impact assessments (EIAs) before commencing any oil and gas project. EIAs help identify potential environmental risks and inform mitigation strategies.

7. **Spill Response Plans:**

- Develop and maintain spill response plans that outline procedures for containing and cleaning up spills. Ensure that response teams are trained and equipped to act swiftly and effectively.

8. **Financial Responsibility:**

- Require operators to demonstrate financial responsibility to cover the costs of response and compensation in the event of a spill. This can include insurance, bonds, or other financial mechanisms.

9. **Continuous Monitoring and Auditing:**

- Implement regular monitoring and auditing of oil and gas operations to verify compliance with safety and spill prevention measures. Independent audits can help identify areas for improvement.

10. **Community Engagement:**

- Engage with local communities and stakeholders to raise awareness about spill risks, involve them in spill prevention efforts, and address their concerns.

11. **Preventive Maintenance:**

- Ensure regular and preventive maintenance of equipment and infrastructure, including pipelines, vessels, and drilling rigs. This helps reduce the risk of equipment failure that can lead to spills.

12. **Real-time Monitoring and Surveillance:**

- Implement real-time monitoring systems that allow for continuous surveillance of operations, enabling rapid detection of abnormal conditions and the immediate initiation of response actions.

13. **Environmental Stewardship:**

- Promote a culture of environmental stewardship and responsible corporate social responsibility. Encourage companies to adopt environmentally sustainable practices and technologies.

14. **International Cooperation:**

- Collaborate with neighboring countries, international organizations, and stakeholders to develop joint spill prevention and response strategies, particularly in areas with shared waters or transboundary environmental risks.

15. **Research and Development:**

- Invest in research and development to improve spill prevention and response technologies. Encourage innovation to address spill challenges effectively.

By implementing these international best practices, countries and industries can significantly reduce the risk of oil and gas spillages and their associated environmental and economic consequences. It is essential to maintain a proactive approach to spill prevention and continually adapt to evolving risks and technologies.

- **The Use of Environmental Impact Assessments**

Environmental Impact Assessments (EIAs) are crucial tools in environmental management and decision-making processes. They are used to evaluate the potential environmental, social, and economic consequences of proposed projects, policies, or activities before they are approved or implemented. The use of EIAs helps to ensure sustainable development, protect ecosystems, and prevent or mitigate adverse impacts. Here are key applications of Environmental Impact Assessments:

1. **Project Development:**

- EIAs are commonly used to assess the potential environmental impacts of various projects, including infrastructure development (such as roads, bridges, and airports), industrial facilities, energy projects (e.g., power plants), and commercial or residential developments.

2. **Natural Resource Management:**

• In natural resource management, EIAs are applied to activities like mining, logging, and agriculture to evaluate their potential impacts on ecosystems, water quality, soil, and biodiversity.

3. **Land Use Planning:**

• Municipal and regional governments use EIAs to assess the environmental implications of proposed land-use plans, zoning changes, and urban development projects.

4. **Policy Development:**

• When governments develop policies and regulations that may have environmental consequences, EIAs help identify and address potential impacts, ensuring that policies are in line with sustainable development goals.

5. **Transportation Planning:**

• EIAs are used to evaluate the environmental effects of transportation projects, including new roads, public transit systems, and airports. This includes assessing traffic emissions, noise, and habitat disruption.

6. **Waste Management:**

- Assessments are conducted to determine the potential environmental consequences of waste management strategies, landfill expansion, and waste-to-energy projects.

7. Water Resource Management:

- EIAs are applied to projects related to water resource management, such as dam construction, water diversion, and wastewater treatment facilities.

8. Renewable Energy Projects:

- Before the construction of renewable energy projects like wind farms, solar installations, and hydropower facilities, EIAs are used to analyze their environmental and social effects.

9. Coastal and Marine Management:

- Coastal and marine EIAs are conducted to assess activities that may affect marine ecosystems, including fishing, aquaculture, and coastal development.

10. Biodiversity Conservation:

- Conservation efforts may require EIAs to assess the potential impacts of habitat restoration, invasive species control, or the reintroduction of endangered species.

11. International Development Projects:

- International organizations and donor agencies often require EIAs for development projects in recipient countries to ensure that environmental and social concerns are addressed.

12. **Environmental Compliance:**

- In many jurisdictions, EIAs are required to obtain permits and approvals for certain activities, and compliance with the EIA process is mandatory.

13. **Public Awareness and Participation:**

- EIAs provide opportunities for public input and engagement, allowing affected communities and stakeholders to voice concerns and influence decision-making.

14. **Conflict Resolution:**

- EIAs can help resolve disputes and conflicts by providing objective information on the potential impacts of a project or policy, allowing stakeholders to reach a consensus.

15. **Adaptive Management:**

- Over the lifecycle of a project, EIAs are used for ongoing monitoring, assessment, and adaptive management to address changing environmental conditions and impacts.

EIAs contribute to informed decision-making, helping authorities and stakeholders weigh the benefits and risks of proposed actions. They also encourage the adoption of mitigation measures and alternatives that minimize adverse environmental effects and promote sustainability. As a result, EIAs play a critical role in fostering environmentally responsible and socially accountable development and policy implementation.

• **Environmental Audits and Monitoring Systems**

Environmental audits and monitoring systems are essential tools for assessing and managing environmental performance. They help organizations, governments, and industries track their environmental impact, compliance with regulations, and progress toward sustainability goals. Here's an overview of environmental audits and monitoring systems:

Environmental Audits:

1. **Definition:** An environmental audit is a systematic assessment of an organization's activities, operations, and facilities to evaluate their compliance with environmental laws, regulations, and standards. It also assesses environmental performance and identifies areas for improvement.

2. **Scope:** Environmental audits can cover various aspects, including air and water quality, waste management, energy efficiency, land use, and biodiversity conservation. They can be comprehensive or focus on specific environmental issues.

3. **Objectives:**

- Assess compliance with environmental laws and regulations.

- Identify areas of non-compliance or potential environmental risks.

- Evaluate the effectiveness of environmental management systems and policies.

- Provide recommendations for improving environmental performance.

- Enhance transparency and accountability.

4. **Types of Environmental Audits:**

- **Compliance Audits:** These audits assess an organization's adherence to environmental laws and regulations.

- **Management System Audits:** They evaluate the effectiveness of an organization's environmental management systems (e.g., ISO 14001) and sustainable practices.

- **Performance Audits:** These audits assess an organization's environmental impact, sustainability, and resource use.

- **Due Diligence Audits:** Conducted before mergers, acquisitions, or real estate transactions to assess potential environmental liabilities.

5. **Benefits:**

- Ensures regulatory compliance.

- Identifies opportunities for cost savings and resource efficiency.

- Enhances public and stakeholder trust.

- Reduces the risk of environmental incidents and liabilities.

- Demonstrates a commitment to sustainability.

Environmental Monitoring Systems:

1. **Definition:** Environmental monitoring systems involve the systematic collection, analysis, and interpretation of data related to environmental parameters such as air quality, water quality, soil conditions, biodiversity, and climate change.

2. **Components of Monitoring Systems:**

- **Data Collection:** Use of sensors, instruments, and sampling techniques to collect data on environmental conditions.

- **Data Analysis:** Interpretation of collected data to assess trends, changes, or anomalies.

- **Reporting:** Communicating monitoring results to stakeholders, authorities, and the public.

- **Feedback Loop:** Using monitoring data to inform decision-making and improve environmental management.

3. **Types of Environmental Monitoring Systems:**

- **Continuous Monitoring:** Real-time data collection using automated sensors for parameters like air quality, water flow, and temperature.

- **Periodic Monitoring:** Sampling and analysis at regular intervals to assess parameters like groundwater quality or wildlife populations.

- **Remote Sensing:** Use of satellite imagery and aerial surveys to monitor large-scale environmental changes.

- **Biodiversity Monitoring:** Tracking changes in species populations, habitat health, and ecosystems.

4. **Applications:**

- **Air and Water Quality Monitoring:** Assessing pollutants and pollutants in the atmosphere and water bodies.

- **Climate Monitoring:** Tracking temperature, precipitation, and greenhouse gas levels.

- **Ecosystem Monitoring:** Evaluating the health and diversity of ecosystems.

- **Industrial Process Monitoring:** Monitoring emissions, waste management, and resource consumption in industrial facilities.

- **Public Health and Safety Monitoring:** Monitoring radiation levels, disease vectors, and other threats to public health.

5. **Benefits:**

- Early detection of environmental issues or hazards.

- Improved resource management and conservation.

- Informed decision-making for environmental protection.

- Verification of compliance with environmental standards.

- Support for research and policy development.

Environmental audits and monitoring systems are integral to environmental protection and sustainable development. They help organizations and governments proactively address environmental challenges, minimize negative impacts, and make data-driven decisions for a more sustainable future.

CHAPTER 7
RESPONSE AND REMEDIATION

- **International Response Mechanisms**

International response mechanisms are structures and frameworks designed to facilitate coordinated, timely, and effective responses to global challenges and crises. These mechanisms bring together countries, organizations, and stakeholders to address issues that transcend national boundaries. Here are some key international response mechanisms in various fields:

1. **Humanitarian Response:**

- **United Nations Office for the Coordination of Humanitarian Affairs (OCHA):** OCHA coordinates international humanitarian response efforts during crises, including natural disasters and conflicts.

- **United Nations High Commissioner for Refugees (UNHCR):** UNHCR leads and coordinates international responses to refugee and displacement crises.

- **International Federation of Red Cross and Red Crescent Societies (IFRC):** IFRC coordinates disaster response and humanitarian assistance through national Red Cross and Red Crescent Societies.

2. **Public Health Response:**

• **World Health Organization (WHO):** WHO leads international responses to public health emergencies and pandemics, including the COVID-19 response.

• **Gavi, the Vaccine Alliance:** Gavi supports the equitable distribution of vaccines to combat preventable diseases globally.

3. **Disaster Response and Relief:**

• **United Nations Disaster Assessment and Coordination (UNDAC):** UNDAC provides rapid response teams for disaster-affected countries to assess needs and coordinate relief efforts.

• **International Search and Rescue Advisory Group (INSARAG):** INSARAG sets standards for urban search and rescue teams deployed to disaster-stricken areas.

4. **Conflict Resolution and Peacekeeping:**

• **United Nations Peacekeeping Operations:** UN peacekeeping missions are deployed to conflict zones to maintain peace and stability.

- **African Union (AU) Peace and Security Council:** The AU intervenes in conflicts across Africa and supports peacekeeping missions.

5. **Environmental and Climate Response:**

- **United Nations Framework Convention on Climate Change (UNFCCC):** UNFCCC leads international efforts to combat climate change, including the Paris Agreement.

- **Intergovernmental Panel on Climate Change (IPCC):** IPCC assesses scientific evidence on climate change and informs global climate policies.

6. **Economic and Financial Response:**

- **International Monetary Fund (IMF):** IMF provides financial assistance to countries facing economic crises and supports macroeconomic stability.

- **World Bank Group:** The World Bank offers financial and technical assistance for development projects in crisis-affected regions.

7. **Migration and Refugee Response:**

- **United Nations Migration Network (UNMN):** UNMN coordinates efforts on migration issues, including refugee and migrant response.

- **International Organization for Migration (IOM):** IOM supports governments and communities in managing migration challenges.

8. **Cybersecurity and Cyber Incident Response:**

- **Forum of Incident Response and Security Teams (FIRST):** FIRST connects global cybersecurity teams to respond to cyber incidents.

- **United Nations Group of Governmental Experts (UN GGE) on Developments in the Field of Information and Telecommunications in the Context of International Security:** UN GGE addresses cybersecurity threats and norms in cyberspace.

9. **Trade and Economic Crises:**

- **World Trade Organization (WTO):** WTO manages international trade disputes and negotiations, promoting global trade stability.

10. **Nuclear and Non-Proliferation Response:**

- **International Atomic Energy Agency (IAEA):** IAEA verifies the peaceful use of nuclear technology and monitors nuclear non-proliferation agreements.

These international response mechanisms play a critical role in addressing global challenges, whether they involve humanitarian crises, public health emergencies, environmental issues, conflict resolution, or economic stability. Their effectiveness depends on collaboration, cooperation, and the commitment of member states and organizations to work together for the common good of humanity.

- **Cross-Border Cooperation**

Cross-border cooperation, often referred to as transboundary cooperation, is a collaborative approach involving neighboring regions or countries working together to address common challenges, harness opportunities, and promote sustainable development. Such cooperation is vital for managing shared resources, resolving cross-border issues, and fostering economic, social, and environmental well-being. Here are key aspects of cross-border cooperation:

1. **Shared Resource Management:**

- Neighboring regions often share natural resources, such as rivers, forests, or fisheries. Cross-border cooperation frameworks help manage and conserve these resources sustainably.

- Example: The Mekong River Commission, involving multiple Southeast Asian countries, collaborates to manage the Mekong River's resources and mitigate shared water-related challenges.

2. **Infrastructure and Connectivity:**

- Cross-border infrastructure projects, such as roads, bridges, and transportation networks, enhance connectivity and facilitate trade, tourism, and economic growth.

- Example: The European Union's Trans-European Transport Network (TEN-T) program supports infrastructure development to connect European regions.

3. **Trade and Economic Integration:**

- Bilateral or multilateral trade agreements and economic cooperation zones promote cross-border trade, investment, and economic integration.

- Example: The East African Community (EAC) facilitates economic integration among its member states, promoting trade and cross-border investments.

4. **Environmental Protection:**

- Cross-border environmental cooperation addresses pollution, conservation, and ecosystem management in areas that span multiple jurisdictions.

- Example: The Commission for Environmental Cooperation (CEC) collaborates among Canada, Mexico, and the United States to address environmental issues in North America.

5. **Healthcare and Disease Control:**

•   Collaboration in healthcare and disease control efforts is essential for addressing cross-border health threats, such as pandemics and the spread of infectious diseases.

•   Example: The European Centre for Disease Prevention and Control (ECDC) supports European countries in monitoring and responding to public health threats.

6. **Conflict Resolution:**

•   Cross-border cooperation can help resolve conflicts or tensions between neighboring regions or countries through dialogue, diplomacy, and confidence-building measures.

•   Example: The Organization for Security and Co-operation in Europe (OSCE) fosters cooperative security and conflict prevention among European and Eurasian states.

7. **Cultural Exchange and Education:**

•   Cultural and educational exchanges across borders promote mutual understanding and people-to-people cooperation.

•   Example: The Fulbright Program facilitates academic and cultural exchanges between the United States and other countries.

8. **Security and Border Management:**

- Cross-border security cooperation can involve sharing intelligence, border management, and collaborative efforts to combat transnational threats like terrorism and organized crime.

- Example: The European Border and Coast Guard Agency (Frontex) enhances security and border control in the European Union.

9. **Emergency Response and Disaster Management:**

- Neighboring regions often collaborate on emergency response and disaster management, sharing resources and expertise during crises.

- Example: The Caribbean Disaster Emergency Management Agency (CDEMA) coordinates disaster response in the Caribbean region.

10. **Legal and Regulatory Harmonization:**

- Cross-border cooperation may involve aligning legal and regulatory frameworks to facilitate trade, investment, and governance across borders.

- Example: The Association of Southeast Asian Nations (ASEAN) works to harmonize regulations and standards among its member states.

Effective cross-border cooperation requires trust, communication, and shared goals among participating regions or countries. It can significantly enhance regional stability, economic growth, environmental sustainability, and overall well-being by addressing common challenges and capitalizing on shared opportunities.

- **Lessons Learned from Past Spillages**

Learning from past spillages is essential to prevent future incidents, improve response efforts, and minimize environmental and economic damage. Several key lessons can be gleaned from past oil and gas spillages:

1. **Preparedness is Crucial:** Spillages can happen at any time and in any location, so preparedness is paramount. Developing and regularly updating spill response plans, conducting drills, and ensuring that personnel are trained in spill response are critical steps.

2. **The Importance of Monitoring and Inspection:** Regular inspection and maintenance of equipment, pipelines, and vessels can help detect potential issues before they lead to a spill. Employing advanced monitoring technologies is also essential.

3. **Environmental Impact is Severe:** Spillages have far-reaching environmental consequences. These incidents harm

aquatic life, disrupt ecosystems, and damage fragile habitats. Therefore, measures to prevent spills must be a top priority.

4. **Human Error Plays a Significant Role:** Many spillages result from human error, whether it's during drilling, transportation, or operational procedures. Emphasizing rigorous safety training and procedures can significantly reduce the risk.

5. **Technological Advancements Aid Response:** New technologies, such as remotely operated vehicles (ROVs) and advanced oil spill response equipment, have improved the effectiveness of response efforts. These technologies enable quicker and more targeted cleanup.

6. **Communication is Key:** Timely and accurate communication with the public, stakeholders, and authorities is essential during a spill. Transparency builds trust, and misinformation or delayed communication can lead to public outrage.

7. **Legal and Regulatory Frameworks Matter:** Having robust legal and regulatory frameworks in place, with strict enforcement and penalties for non-compliance, can deter risky behaviors and hold responsible parties accountable.

8. **Global Cooperation is Necessary:** Many spillages occur in international waters or affect multiple countries. Effective

international cooperation is crucial for managing these incidents and ensuring a coordinated response.

9. **Resource Allocation is Critical:** Adequate funding and resources must be allocated for both prevention and response efforts. This includes investing in research and development to improve spill response technology.

10. **Environmental Remediation is Challenging:** Cleaning up after a spill is a complex and lengthy process. Developing effective cleanup techniques and restoration strategies is an ongoing challenge.

11. **Public Awareness and Engagement:** Involving local communities and stakeholders in spill response and prevention efforts can help raise awareness, gather local knowledge, and enhance public support.

12. **Insurance and Financial Responsibility:** Requiring operators to demonstrate financial responsibility is essential. Ensuring that they have the financial means to cover the costs of response and compensation helps protect affected parties.

13. **Recycling and Waste Management:** Proper disposal of recovered oil and waste from spill response is vital to prevent further environmental harm. Recycling and waste management plans should be part of response efforts.

14. **Preventing Spill Migration:** Techniques to contain and prevent the spread of oil and gas in the event of a spill, such as the use of booms and skimmers, are essential to minimize environmental damage.

15. **Research and Development:** Continued research and development efforts can lead to the discovery of innovative spill response technologies and more environmentally friendly drilling and transportation methods.

Learning from past spillages is an ongoing process. It requires a commitment to applying lessons learned and continuously improving industry practices, regulations, and response capabilities to reduce the risk of future incidents and their environmental and economic impact.

- **Post-Spill Assessment and Recovery**

Post-spill assessment and recovery efforts are critical phases in the aftermath of an oil and gas spill. These processes aim to evaluate the impact of the spill, rehabilitate affected ecosystems, and help affected communities and industries recover. Here are key steps and considerations in post-spill assessment and recovery:

1. **Environmental Impact Assessment:**

- Conduct a thorough assessment of the spill's environmental impact, including damage to ecosystems, wildlife, water quality, and air quality.

- Evaluate the long-term effects on habitats, species, and biodiversity.

2. Resource Damage Assessment (RDA):

- Calculate the extent of damage to natural resources, such as fisheries, wetlands, and recreational areas.

- Determine the compensation required for the restoration of these resources.

3. Health and Safety Assessment:

- Assess the potential health impacts on affected communities, cleanup workers, and responders.

- Monitor air, water, and soil quality to ensure that no lingering health hazards exist.

4. Economic Impact Analysis:

- Evaluate the spill's economic impact on local industries, including fisheries, tourism, and real estate.

- Assess job losses and reduced property values.

5. Compensation and Liability:

- Identify responsible parties and enforce liability for the spill.

- Ensure that the responsible entities provide compensation to affected parties, such as fishermen, tourism businesses, and property owners.

6. **Rehabilitation and Restoration:**

- Develop and implement habitat restoration and rehabilitation plans to help affected ecosystems recover.

- Implement measures to promote the recovery of fish and wildlife populations.

7. **Monitoring and Adaptive Management:**

- Continuously monitor the recovery of ecosystems and natural resources.

- Adjust rehabilitation efforts based on ongoing assessments and evolving conditions.

8. **Community Recovery:**

- Provide support and assistance to affected communities to help them recover economically and socially.

- Develop programs to stimulate local economies and job creation.

9.   **Educational and Outreach Programs:**

•   Conduct public education and outreach programs to inform communities about ongoing recovery efforts and health risks.

•   Promote environmental stewardship and sustainable practices.

10. **Research and Innovation:**

•   Invest in research and development to find innovative and environmentally friendly solutions for spill recovery and prevention.

•   Foster collaboration between academia, industry, and government to advance spill response technologies.

11. **Regulatory and Policy Improvements:**

•   Review and update regulatory frameworks and policies to enhance spill prevention and response measures.

•   Ensure that lessons learned from the spill are incorporated into these improvements.

12. **Long-Term Monitoring and Planning:**

•   Develop long-term monitoring programs to assess the lasting effects of the spill.

- Establish a plan for long-term recovery and ecosystem health.

13. **Community Engagement and Consultation:**

- Involve local communities and stakeholders in recovery decision-making and planning.

- Seek input and feedback to address their concerns and needs.

14. **International Collaboration:**

- Engage in international collaboration and data sharing, especially for spills that impact multiple countries or regions.

- Coordinate efforts to address cross-border environmental issues.

15. **Communication and Transparency:**

- Maintain open and transparent communication with affected communities, the public, and stakeholders.

- Keep them informed about the progress of recovery efforts and any ongoing risks.

Post-spill assessment and recovery require a multi-pronged approach that involves government agencies, environmental organizations, industry stakeholders, and affected communities. The goal is to restore affected areas, minimize long-term

118

environmental harm, support economic recovery, and ensure that valuable lessons from the spill are applied to prevent future incidents.

- **The Role of Indigenous Communities in Remediation**

The role of indigenous communities in remediation efforts following oil and gas spillages is crucial. Indigenous communities often have an intimate connection to the affected land, water, and ecosystems and possess traditional knowledge that can be invaluable for effective and culturally sensitive recovery. Here are key aspects of their role in remediation:

1. **Traditional Ecological Knowledge (TEK):**

- Indigenous communities have deep-rooted knowledge of local ecosystems, including the behavior of species, plant medicines, and traditional land use practices.

- TEK can be applied to assess the environmental impact of spills, identify areas in need of restoration, and guide recovery efforts.

2. **Cultural and Spiritual Connections:**

- Indigenous communities have cultural and spiritual connections to the land and water, making them stewards of their territories.

- Their values and beliefs often prioritize environmental preservation, which aligns with remediation goals.

3. **Collaboration and Consultation:**

- Engage in meaningful consultation and collaboration with indigenous communities to ensure their perspectives and needs are considered in remediation planning and decision-making.

- Recognize and respect their rights to land and resources as well as their sovereignty.

4. **Participation in Assessment and Planning:**

- Involve indigenous communities in environmental impact assessments, damage assessments, and the development of remediation plans.

- Incorporate indigenous perspectives and priorities into the decision-making process.

5. **Capacity Building:**

- Support capacity building within indigenous communities by providing training and resources to enable their active participation in remediation efforts.

- This includes technical training for community members and support for community-led projects.

6. **On-the-Ground Involvement:**

• Facilitate the active involvement of indigenous community members in the hands-on work of spill recovery, such as habitat restoration and wildlife protection efforts.

• Ensure that local communities benefit from employment and economic opportunities related to remediation.

7. **Cultural Resources Protection:**

• Take steps to protect cultural resources and heritage sites that may be affected by the spill and remediation activities.

• Work collaboratively with indigenous communities to safeguard these sites.

8. **Traditional Practices Integration:**

• Integrate traditional practices and knowledge into remediation strategies, where applicable and culturally appropriate.

• Utilize traditional methods for land and water restoration, such as controlled burns and plantings of native species.

9. **Monitoring and Evaluation:**

• Engage indigenous communities in the long-term monitoring and evaluation of remediation efforts to ensure that the recovery is sustainable and culturally sensitive.

- Adapt plans as necessary based on their observations and insights.

10. **Knowledge Exchange:**

- Foster a two-way knowledge exchange between indigenous communities and technical experts, researchers, and government agencies.

- Recognize the value of indigenous knowledge in enhancing the effectiveness of remediation strategies.

11. **Community Well-Being and Health:**

- Address the potential health and well-being impacts on indigenous communities resulting from spills and remediation efforts.

- Provide support for physical and mental health services as needed.

12. **Legal Recognition and Agreements:**

- Ensure that indigenous rights, land tenure, and legal agreements, such as treaties and land claims, are respected and upheld throughout the remediation process.

13. **Restorative Justice and Compensation:**

- Implement restorative justice approaches that take into account the harm caused to indigenous communities and their lands.

- Provide fair compensation for damages and losses.

14. **Education and Awareness:**

- Educate all stakeholders, including the public, about the importance of indigenous perspectives and the contributions of indigenous communities in spill recovery efforts.

15. **Cultural Protocols and Respect:**

- Observe cultural protocols and practices, such as acknowledging traditional territories and obtaining consent for land use.

- Show respect for indigenous languages, ceremonies, and customs.

The role of indigenous communities in remediation is not just a matter of environmental justice but also a recognition of the wisdom, resilience, and resourcefulness they bring to these efforts. By incorporating indigenous knowledge and fostering collaboration, remediation efforts can be more effective, culturally sensitive, and sustainable.

CHAPTER 8
DISPUTE RESOLUTION AND
ADJUDICATION

- **International Courts and Tribunals**

International courts and tribunals are legal bodies that provide a forum for the resolution of disputes between states, individuals, or organizations in the context of international law. These institutions play a crucial role in maintaining global order, upholding the rule of law, and settling international conflicts peacefully. Some notable international courts and tribunals include:

- **International Court of Justice (ICJ):** The ICJ, often referred to as the World Court, is the principal judicial organ of the United Nations. It settles legal disputes between states and provides advisory opinions on legal questions referred by UN bodies and specialized agencies.

- **International Criminal Court (ICC):** The ICC prosecutes individuals for the most serious international crimes, including genocide, war crimes, and crimes against humanity. While not directly related to oil and gas, it addresses grave violations of international law that can occur in conflict regions with resource interests.

- **Permanent Court of Arbitration (PCA):** The PCA is a forum for resolving international disputes through arbitration and other forms of dispute resolution. It is often used for commercial and investment disputes.

- **International Tribunal for the Law of the Sea (ITLOS):** ITLOS deals with disputes related to the interpretation and application of the United Nations Convention on the Law of the Sea (UNCLOS), which includes issues concerning maritime boundaries, environmental protection, and resource exploitation.

International courts and tribunals are crucial in the context of oil and gas when disputes arise between states, multinational corporations, and international stakeholders regarding issues like territorial boundaries, resource exploration, environmental damage, and treaty violations.

2. State-to-State Dispute Settlement:

State-to-state dispute settlement refers to the processes by which countries resolve conflicts and disagreements in the international arena. These disputes can encompass a wide range of issues, including territorial disputes, trade disagreements, environmental concerns, and more. The methods for state-to-state dispute resolution typically include:

- **Negotiation:** Countries may seek to resolve disputes through direct negotiations or diplomatic channels. Negotiation can involve compromise and bilateral or multilateral discussions.

- **Mediation:** In some cases, a third party, often a neutral mediator or international organization, may facilitate negotiations between disputing states to help them reach an agreement.

- **Arbitration:** Arbitration involves submitting a dispute to an impartial tribunal, whose decision is legally binding. Arbitral awards can resolve disputes in a less adversarial setting than litigation.

- **Adjudication:** Some disputes are brought before international courts or tribunals, as mentioned earlier. These judicial bodies issue judgments that states are typically bound to follow.

State-to-state dispute settlement mechanisms are highly relevant in the context of oil and gas when countries are contesting issues like maritime boundaries, resource rights, or environmental damage stemming from the energy sector.

3. Investor-State Disputes:

Investor-state disputes occur when a foreign investor or corporation initiates legal proceedings against a host state. These disputes typically arise from violations of international investment agreements, trade agreements, or investment protection treaties. In the context of the oil and gas industry, investor-state disputes can occur when multinational energy companies encounter unfavorable treatment by host states. Key elements of investor-state disputes include:

- **Investor Protection Treaties:** Bilateral investment treaties (BITs), multilateral agreements, and free trade agreements often contain provisions that protect foreign investors from discriminatory or unfair treatment by host states.

- **Arbitration:** Investor-state disputes are frequently resolved through international arbitration, often under the rules of organizations such as the International Centre for Settlement of Investment Disputes (ICSID).

- **Claims:** Foreign investors may bring claims against host states for actions that affect their investments, such as expropriation, breach of contract, or regulatory changes that negatively impact their operations.

- **Compensation:** If an arbitral tribunal finds in favor of the investor, the host state may be required to pay compensation for damages or lost investments.

Investor-state disputes are pertinent to the oil and gas sector, given the substantial international investments and the potential for conflicts arising from regulatory changes, expropriation, or breaches of investment agreements.

These mechanisms for resolving international disputes, whether they involve states, investors, or organizations, are critical for maintaining international stability, promoting adherence to international law, and ensuring that grievances are addressed through peaceful means rather than escalating into conflicts.

- **Mediation and Arbitration**

- **Mediation:** Mediation is a form of alternative dispute resolution (ADR) in which a neutral third party, known as the mediator, assists parties in resolving their disputes. The mediator does not make a decision but facilitates communication and negotiation between the parties. In the context of international environmental disputes, mediation can be used to find mutually acceptable solutions to issues such as transboundary pollution, resource management, or environmental treaty compliance. It is a collaborative and consensual approach to conflict resolution.

- **Arbitration:** Arbitration is another ADR method, but in this case, a neutral third party, the arbitrator or arbitral tribunal, renders a legally binding decision based on the evidence and arguments presented by the parties. Arbitration can be employed in international environmental disputes when parties have agreed to resolve their disagreements through this process. It provides a more structured and formal mechanism compared to mediation.

2. Emerging Trends in International Environmental Dispute Resolution:

- **Increased Use of Mediation:** Mediation is gaining prominence in international environmental dispute resolution due to its non-adversarial nature and the potential for preserving long-term relationships between states and stakeholders. Environmental treaties and conventions often include provisions encouraging mediation before arbitration or litigation.

- **Customary and Soft Law Frameworks:** Customary international law and soft law instruments, such as non-binding principles and guidelines, are increasingly utilized to address environmental disputes. These flexible frameworks allow for innovative approaches to resolving complex environmental challenges.

- **Private Sector Involvement:** As the role of the private sector in environmental matters grows, there is a trend towards involving corporations, industries, and NGOs in international environmental dispute resolution processes. Public-private partnerships and collaborative efforts are being explored to address environmental issues.

- **Multi-Tiered Dispute Resolution Mechanisms:** Environmental disputes often involve multiple layers of jurisdiction and complexity. Multi-tiered dispute resolution mechanisms, including mechanisms within international agreements, are being designed to address these complexities efficiently.

- **Enhanced Access to Justice:** There is a growing recognition of the importance of ensuring access to justice for affected communities and individuals in environmental disputes. This trend emphasizes the involvement of local stakeholders and the broader public in dispute resolution processes.

- **Environmental Impact Assessment (EIA) and Early Warning Systems:** The use of EIA and early warning systems to prevent environmental disputes is becoming more prevalent. These tools help identify potential environmental risks and conflicts before they escalate.

- **Integration of Scientific and Technical Expertise:** Given the technical nature of many environmental disputes, there is a trend towards incorporating scientific and technical experts into dispute resolution processes to provide informed assessments and solutions.

- **Cyber-Mediation and Online Dispute Resolution:** The digital age has introduced new opportunities for resolving environmental disputes online, often referred to as cyber-mediation and online dispute resolution (ODR). These methods can facilitate negotiations and resolution without the need for physical meetings.

- **Climate Change Disputes:** As climate change becomes a central issue in international relations, there is a growing focus on resolving climate-related disputes. New mechanisms and frameworks are being developed to address disputes related to emissions reductions, adaptation measures, and loss and damage.

- **Transboundary Water Disputes:** The growing competition for water resources in transboundary river basins has led to an increased emphasis on resolving water-related disputes through international frameworks and cooperative agreements.

These emerging trends reflect the evolving nature of international environmental dispute resolution, driven by the need to address complex environmental challenges, ensure equitable access to justice, and adapt to technological advancements. It is essential for international environmental law and policy to remain flexible and responsive to these developments to effectively address environmental issues on a global scale.

CHAPTER 9
FUTURE DIRECTIONS AND CHALLENGES

- **Future Directions and Challenges**

As the world grapples with the complexities of balancing energy demand, environmental sustainability, and economic growth, the oil and gas industry finds itself at the crossroads of unprecedented change. Future directions for this sector are being shaped by a confluence of factors, from the global push for cleaner and more sustainable energy sources to the evolving landscape of regulations and social responsibility.

1. Energy Transition: One of the most significant trends on the horizon is the ongoing transition to renewable and sustainable energy sources. As the world's awareness of climate change intensifies, governments, industries, and consumers are seeking cleaner alternatives. This transition poses a considerable challenge to the oil and gas sector, as it requires a shift in focus from traditional fossil fuels to renewable energy technologies.

2. Environmental Regulations: Environmental regulations are expected to become increasingly stringent in the coming years. Governments and international bodies are tightening their oversight of environmental impacts related to oil and gas operations. This shift places a greater onus on the industry to adhere to emissions standards, conduct comprehensive environmental impact assessments, and invest in technologies that minimize their carbon footprint.

3. Technological Innovation: The oil and gas industry has long been associated with cutting-edge technologies. Looking ahead, this sector will continue to innovate to meet new challenges. This includes advancements in clean energy, carbon capture and storage, and enhanced exploration and drilling techniques. Technological innovation is crucial for both improving operational efficiency and reducing environmental impacts.

4. Resource Scarcity: With traditional oil and gas reserves depleting, the industry is turning its attention to securing new sources of these finite resources. This often involves exploration in remote or environmentally sensitive areas, presenting a substantial challenge in terms of environmental preservation and sustainable resource extraction.

5. Environmental and Social Responsibility: The future of the industry also entails a heightened focus on environmental and social responsibility. Oil and gas companies are increasingly expected to demonstrate their commitment to sustainability, community engagement, and transparency. This aligns with the growing influence of public awareness and investor demands for responsible corporate behavior.

6. International Cooperation: Addressing global environmental challenges necessitates international collaboration. The oil and gas industry must work alongside governments and international organizations to tackle issues like cross-border pollution, the protection of shared resources, and climate change mitigation.

7. Environmental Justice: The industry is also recognizing the importance of environmental justice, which encompasses the equitable distribution of environmental burdens and benefits. Addressing the unique concerns of marginalized communities and ensuring that they are not disproportionately affected by environmental challenges is a key consideration.

8. Public Awareness: The industry's future will be shaped by public awareness, environmental education, and advocacy. As communities and individuals become more informed about the environmental impacts of oil and gas operations, they are increasingly influencing government policies and corporate practices.

9. Geopolitical Factors: Geopolitical tensions and global energy dynamics have a significant bearing on the industry. Political disputes and changing alliances can affect the industry's operations, international relations, and resource accessibility.

10. Natural Disasters and Climate Resilience: The industry must also adapt to the increasing frequency and intensity of natural disasters and the impacts of climate change. Building resilience against such events is becoming paramount.

11. Circular Economy and Recycling: The concept of a circular economy, where waste and byproducts are reduced, reused, and recycled, is gaining momentum in the industry. This minimizes environmental impacts by reducing waste and promoting resource efficiency.

12. Innovation in Green Hydrogen and Alternative Fuels: The development of green hydrogen, synthetic fuels, and other alternatives is a response to the need to reduce carbon emissions from the industry. These innovations are crucial in aligning with climate goals and sustainability targets.

13. Decommissioning and Environmental Restoration: As oil and gas sites reach the end of their productive life, the industry is confronted with the challenge of decommissioning and environmental restoration. Properly managing the closure and restoration of these sites is essential for minimizing long-term environmental impacts.

The future directions and challenges of the oil and gas industry are marked by a profound shift toward environmental responsibility, innovation, and a more sustainable energy landscape. This industry, long a cornerstone of global energy supply, is evolving to meet the demands of a changing world, where environmental concerns and sustainable practices take center stage.

CONCLUSION

In the preceding chapters, we embarked on a journey through the multifaceted and ever-evolving landscape of the oil and gas industry. We delved into its historical significance, the complexities of environmental and economic impact, and the intricate tapestry of international law governing its activities. We explored the role of emerging technologies, the challenges of climate change, and the imperatives of sustainable practices.

As we conclude this exploration, it is evident that the oil and gas industry stands at a pivotal juncture, where it must grapple with formidable challenges and embrace transformative change. The future of this industry is inextricably tied to the broader global commitment to environmental sustainability and the quest for a cleaner, more responsible energy future.

The ongoing energy transition towards renewables and the pursuit of cleaner alternatives present formidable challenges to the sector. These challenges are compounded by increasingly stringent environmental regulations and mounting public and investor pressure for responsible corporate behavior. The oil and gas industry faces the dual mandate of meeting energy demand while minimizing its environmental footprint.

Technological innovation has become the linchpin of the industry's response. From advanced sensors and data analytics to carbon capture and storage, innovation is central to improving operational efficiency and reducing environmental impacts. The industry must continue to adapt and innovate to navigate the evolving landscape successfully.

In this journey, the oil and gas industry's role in international cooperation and adherence to strengthened legal frameworks is paramount. Collaborative efforts on a global scale are essential to address cross-border environmental challenges and mitigate the impacts of climate change. These efforts are critical not just for the industry's survival but for the well-being of the planet.

Environmental justice and public awareness have emerged as driving forces shaping the industry's future. Acknowledging the concerns of marginalized communities and engaging with the broader public are not optional but imperative. The industry must be attuned to the aspirations and expectations of a more informed and environmentally-conscious world.

As we gaze into the horizon of this ever-evolving industry, we recognize that its destiny lies in its ability to adapt, innovate, and embrace sustainable practices. The challenges are formidable, but they are matched by the potential for transformation, responsibility, and a more harmonious coexistence with the environment.

The oil and gas industry is not just an energy source; it is a catalyst for change. Its future will be shaped by its capacity to navigate the complex web of environmental, economic, and social dynamics. The chapters of this book have offered insights, analysis, and considerations to help guide this journey towards a more responsible and sustainable future.

In the coming years, as the industry charts new courses and forges new paths, it carries with it the weighty responsibility of securing energy resources for the world while being mindful stewards of our planet. The journey is ongoing, the challenges are formidable, but the destination is a world where energy coexists harmoniously with the environment, where responsibility is paramount, and where the oil and gas industry is an integral part of a cleaner, sustainable, and prosperous global future.